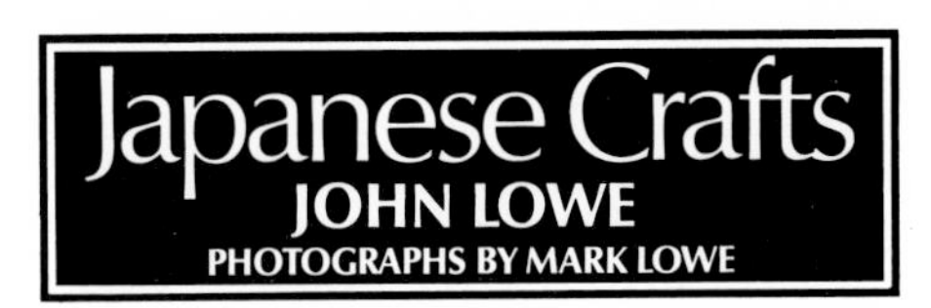
Japanese Crafts
JOHN LOWE
PHOTOGRAPHS BY MARK LOWE

畳 包丁 簾 扇子 風呂敷 櫛 傘

筆 障子 香 提灯 尺八 お茶菓子 お鮨

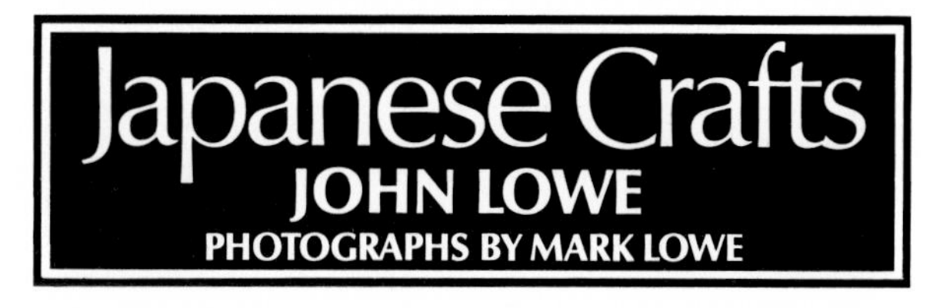

Research Assistant Miss Fumio Watanabe

JOHN MURRAY

To Fumio Watanabe *Best Person*
and to all those craftsmen and
owners of shops and workshops
who made this book possible

Brooms
Shoten Naitō
Daiji Naitō
Yoshio Ishikawa

Carrying Cloths
Hirotsugu Iwagaki
Hideo Nishimura
Yasuhide Watanabe

Combs
Michikazu Takeuchi

Fans
Shinji Miyawaki
Yoshinosuke Miyata
Kitaro Teramura
Tokio Kitazawa

Floor Mats
Hiroshi Kubo

Flutes
Kazan Zenmura

Incense
Shigetaro Hata

Knives
Isao Saito
Teiichiro Yamaguchi

Lanterns
Mitsugu Hiraide

Raw Fish
Yoshihisa Futaya

Seal-Engraving
Clifton Karhu

Sweetmeats
Yoshimasa Ishihara

Umbrellas
Kenichi Fujisawa
Toshikazu Masuda

Writing Brushes
Kusaka-san
Kiyokazu Otuji

First published in Great Britain in 1983
by John Murray (Publishers) Ltd
50 Albemarle Street, London W1X 4BD

This book was designed and produced
by John Calmann and Cooper Ltd, London

Filmset by Keyspools Ltd, Golborne, Lancs.
Printed and bound in Hong Kong
by Mandarin Offset Ltd.

British Library Cataloguing in Publication Data
Lowe, John
Japanese crafts.
1. Handicrafts—Japan—History
I. Title
680 TT105

ISBN 0-7195-4016-X

Contents

A carrying cloth with a simple bamboo design

Acknowledgments

This book hovered about at the back of my mind for several years until it was made a reality by the kindness of John Calmann, shortly before his death. In those earlier years many people, only some of whom I now remember, encouraged my interest in Japanese traditional crafts and taught me about them. There were a few lively discussions with Bernard Leach and a memorable day at Shoji Hamada's pottery. Over many years I have enjoyed both the knowledge and friendship of Tsune Sesoko who is a more reliable guide to traditional Japan than anyone else I know. In Kyoto I frequently received help and kindness from Ishinosuke Mizutani, Shoichiro Mizutani and other members of that large and warm-hearted family. I am also most grateful to Takashi Yanagi. It was Seibu Ltd that first brought me to Japan and my warmest thanks are due to many friends in that great company who first enabled me to visit so many different places; of them special thanks are due to Takao Mori and Shigeo Tanaka. Nor shall I ever forget Akiko Kawade who with equal enthusiasm and discrimination introduced me to Kyoto and its crafts.

Since we began working on the book we have received help from many people, some of whom are listed in the dedication. I could not have undertaken the book had not Doshisha University most kindly offered me a visiting professorship and I would like to offer special thanks to Dr I. Saito and to Dr Kitagaki of the Department of English Literature. A number of my graduate students helped in different ways, among them Hitomi Okamura and Kaoru Imanishi. Special gratitude is also due to Misako Imanishi who acted as our interpreter in the early stages.

Like most really busy people, Clifton Karhu always finds time when help is needed. Apart from being the subject of one chapter and adviser on several others, he did the calligraphy for the *kanji* headings to each chapter. I am most grateful to him, and to his wife, Lois, who always has the answers to my practical problems. Stephen McEnally kindly arranged the introduction to the *tatami* workshop, while Masao Takada made everything possible in Gifu, including a memorable lunch. Without his help there could have been no chapters on lanterns or umbrellas. For constant kindness in Kyoto I would like to thank David and Anne Hale and, not only for great kindness, but also for all she taught me, Mrs Ogata, my landlady at Chotoku-in, sub-temple of Shōkoku-ji, where I so happily lived for my first year in Kyoto.

To my two collaborators more than thanks is due and, in terms of hard work, this book is more theirs than mine. It must always be a special pleasure for a father to work with his son on such a project. In the last stages I was forced to take a few of the photographs myself and it was only then that I fully appreciated what an exacting task I had set Mark, for not only are photographic conditions terrible in most Japanese craft workshops but one is also haunted by the knowledge that there can never be a second chance. Both he and Fumio Watanabe worked on their own initiative and between them overcame every problem. Looking back, I realize that we frequently pushed Fumio into situations that must have been almost unbearable for a Japanese but she grew used to our impatient ways and by one means or another secured the introductions we needed. I thank them both most warmly. The good things in this book are theirs. The errors are mine.

John Lowe
Kyoto 1982

Introduction

Exquisite wrapping is a hall-mark of the famous sweetmeat shops

The Main Periods of Japanese History

JOMON to 200 BC

YAYOI 200 BC to 250 AD

KOFUN 250 to 552

ASUKA 552 to 645

NARA 645 to 794
(Nara was capital of Japan)

HEIAN 794 to 1185
(Kyoto was capital of Japan until end of Edo period)

KAMAKURA 1185 to 1392

MUROMACHI 1392 to 1568

MOMOYAMA 1568 to 1600

EDO 1600 to 1867

MEIJI 1868 to 1912
(Edo was made capital and name changed to Tokyo)

TAISHO 1912 to 1926

SHOWA 1926 to the present

Japanese crafts were much admired by early foreign visitors to Japan in the second half of the nineteenth century, for their design, their quality and their beauty. Indeed, the earliest European and American writers were so beguiled by the crafts that, while their books devoted hundreds of pages to *netsuke* and basketwork, Japanese painting and sculpture were dismissed in a few pages as hardly worthy of attention. This unbalanced attitude, which to some extent persists in Europe, was once nicely described as being like 'judging the Italian Renaissance by a piece of Venetian glass'.

It has been mainly American scholars, from about 1900, who have restored a balance and at the same time have showed that in Japan no hard line is drawn between art and craft, or between artists and craftsmen. The Japanese artist is first a craftsman, and the greatest Japanese artists have never hesitated to decorate humble craft objects. Japanese traditional crafts have continued to flourish and to remain at the heart of Japanese daily life at every level of society. And this despite the ever-accelerating modernization of Japan during the past hundred years.

This book examines Japanese crafts and craftsmanship today, from different but related points of view. Fourteen different traditional crafts were chosen, because they illustrated both a wide range of Japanese craftsmanship and also various aspects of everyday life in Japan today, in which all these crafts continue to play some part. The craft and craftsman are dealt with in the second part of each chapter, where the craft process is described in detail, accompanied by action photographs. It is hoped that these craft descriptions will be of particular interest to practising Western craftsmen and women, professional or amateur, and to craft teachers. For them, a brief 'practical note' is added to suitable crafts. The first part of each chapter gives a brief history of the craft, describes something of its place in Japanese life, past and present, and uses it to illustrate certain Japanese attitudes, trying to show that this miscellaneous collection of craft objects are not social relics, but an integral part of Japanese social life. To the foreigner these objects have an exotic quality. But to understand them properly one must remember that to the Japanese they are as much a part of daily life as their rice-cooker or their raincoat. And it must also be remembered that the fourteen crafts described here are only a small proportion of the traditional Japanese crafts still flourishing in Japan.

How and why has this large number of traditional crafts continued to play a real part in modern Japanese daily life, in a society which is becoming among the most advanced in the world? Each week new statistics show the increase in car ownership, and in the number of television sets, video equipment, washing machines and other applied technology per Japanese household. There is no doubt that Japan is in the forefront of the micro-chip age. Despite this massive modernization and the Japanese craving for novelty and new electronic gadgetry, it is likely that in most Japanese homes one would find at least two or three of the traditional objects described in this book, and in regular use. Few houses are without one *tatami*-room; millions of Japanese women and young girls still learn and practise tea ceremony; every Japanese must have a seal; no restaurant is without traditional knives and few streets without at least one paper lantern. Japan is unique in many ways, but most obviously in this extraordinary mixture of extremely old and extremely new.

Basically, the Japanese are probably the most conservative people in the world. This extreme conservatism is rooted in their overwhelming desire for security which for the majority of Japanese overrides every other consideration in life. In the tight structure of Japanese society, there is little room for the individual to manoeuvre. This is a matter of both physical and psychological lack of space. For most Japanese there is no life outside society and the preservation of society therefore ensures the continuation of security. Tradition remains an essential reality in such a society, and the continuation of traditional activities as an integral part of life ensures that traditional crafts retain a 'living place' in life, and do not, as in most other places, become the government-subsidised toys of tourism.

The small selection of crafts in this book shows how traditional crafts are a part of every side of Japanese life: the Shinto shrine and Buddhist temple, the festivals, old rituals such as tea ceremony, social occasions and customs, dress, food, entertainment and the most humdrum activities of home life. The word 'craft' tends to conjure up an image of the 'rustic' and thoughts of folk art. There is splendid folk art and craft in Japan, but the traditional crafts considered here are separate, and in no sense 'rustic'. These are mostly sophisticated objects, made by a craft refined by centuries of experience. They are not only fascinating in the social purpose they serve but, compared with craftwork anywhere else in the world, of exceptional beauty.

It may throw some light on both the Japanese craft world and on Japanese life to describe a few of the difficulties we had in putting this book together. We were all living in Kyoto and the book is based on the work of Kyoto craftsmen, except for umbrellas and lanterns which are a speciality of Gifu. Many of these objects are made elsewhere in Japan but Kyoto remains the great centre of traditional crafts. Traditional crafts are as much a subject of interest to the Japanese public as to any foreign admirer, and for this reason well-known Japanese and particularly Kyoto craftsmen are besieged by the Japanese 'media' who, while providing welcome publicity, also take up a great deal of these craftsmen's time. They are therefore becoming reluctant to allow visitors into their workshops, particularly foreigners – a book published in the West is not going to affect craft sales in Kyoto!

Partly to overcome this basic resistance, but more because nothing can be done in Japan without an introduction, by far our biggest problem was to obtain the necessary introductions, either directly to craftsmen, or to well-known shops who would introduce us to the craftsmen working for them. And thereby hang several tales, of which I shall tell two.

I started with the slight advantage that I was a visiting professor at Doshisha, Kyoto's largest and best-known private university. In Japanese society, unless you are a famous artist, you can have no individual identity, only the identity of the organization to which you belong. So at least I had an academic identity, albeit a humble one. But in no way did this identity entitle me to pick up the telephone and start trying to make appointments. We were helpless without the right introductions, and here an almost intolerable burden fell on Fumio Watanabe who did all the legwork, spadework – and dirty work! Let me give one example.

Her father is a doctor and through him Fumio got in touch with a powerful pharmaceutical company who most helpfully gave us an excellent introduction to Shoeido, the famous incense-makers of Kyoto. Shigetaro Hata-san was extremely kind and helpful and we got everything we needed. Because this had gone so well, Fumio decided to ask the pharmaceutical company if they would help with a second introduction. She returned hot-faced and miserable from the telephone. It had been made extremely clear to her, in an oblique Japanese way, that while her father's business with the company rated one introduction, it most certainly did not rate two!

I am glad to say that I was the victim of this second tale. I knew that we should have to visit Gifu to study the making of umbrellas and paper lanterns but we had no contacts there and were stuck for introductions. As a last resort I thought of a well-known professor at one of Kyoto's best universities, who is a leading authority on Japanese traditional crafts. I thought I might ask him this favour as I had recently given a talk to a seminar of his on a totally different subject. I approached the professor through one of his acolytes. The acolyte took an unenthusiastic view; I should need to spend weeks in Gifu to make such a study; such introductions were extremely difficult to make; and, by implication, the request was a waste of time as no foreigner could ever understand the intricacies of making either Japanese lanterns or umbrellas. There followed a long silence, but I persisted with the occasional telephone call. After several weeks I received a rather grubby piece of paper with two names written on it; no addresses and no telephone numbers. I suppose it was to be considered some kind of face-saving device?

By chance I was having dinner with Clifton Karhu that evening and I told him of my 'defeat'. Stupidly, I had completely forgotten that Clif had lived in Gifu when he first settled in Japan. 'No problem. Can you give me until tomorrow?' he asked. Since we had just wasted about eight weeks, that seemed reasonable. The next afternoon he telephoned. 'Can you be on the six-thirty train tomorrow? My friend, Masao Takada-san, will meet you at Gifu station in his car and will see that you get everything you want.' Thanks to the great and imaginative kindness of Takada-san we saw everything we needed in one day and late that night returned to Kyoto with pages of notes and hundreds of photographs. There are many morals to this tale, not least, if you want anything in Japan, first ask a foreigner!

To some extent this expert, and other Japanese experts, do not like anyone trespassing on their ground; however, in fairness I must say that their reluctance is partly due to the fact that most Japanese simply cannot believe that foreigners can understand or come to grips with things Japanese. I remember that when my second son was living in Kyoto, he began to learn the *shakuhachi*. When Japanese friends learned that he had bought a good bamboo flute to take back to England, they said with one voice: 'It will split almost immediately in the English climate'. They were too polite to add their underlying thought that it was all a waste of time anyway as he would never be able to play such a difficult Japanese instrument! Two years later the flute is still in admirable condition, and the playing is not so bad either!

Crafts everywhere, but particularly in Japan, tend to be invested with a certain mystique, not so much by the working craftsmen as by the scholars and specialists who in this way aggrandize their subject. They, and most Japanese, through lack of experience (particularly lack of foreign travel) and because of the particularly narrow view of specialization in Japan, think that everything in Japan is uniquely Japanese and therefore a mystery to the outsider. In some areas this may be true, but in the field of craftsmanship it is not. As I went around the workshops of Kyoto, while delighting in those things uniquely Japanese, I was equally fascinated to find tools and processes related to others I had seen in craftwork all over the world. Sometimes a craftsman would go to great lengths to explain some 'Japanese' process which in fact I had first learned from the village carpenter as a nine-year-old schoolboy in England. Many things in Japan are hard for the foreigner to understand, some things impossible. But that does not mean he has to be excluded from the skilful but wholly understandable processes of traditional crafts.

I must emphasize that once one has penetrated the academic defences to meet the craftsmen themselves, the attitudes are totally different. Throughout this study, and without exception, the craftsmen and owners of workshops were welcoming, kind, direct, and showed us everything we wanted to see with enthusiastic and knowledgeable explanations. Naturally, any craftsman who has spent forty or fifty years perfecting a few processes with skill and dedication, must be tempted slightly to inflate the difficulty of what he is doing. But mostly Japanese craftsmen are unusually modest, incredibly hard-working and extremely responsive to the enthusiasm and interest of any genuine student of their craft.

Japanese craftsmen tend to work long hours, often in cramped and, by modern standards, rather primitive conditions. We were continually amazed at how such immaculate work could emerge from such cluttered workshops. But there is no magic in the high quality of these traditional crafts. Long apprenticeship, a high standard of skill deepened by experience, extreme dedication, discipline and, above all else, a high degree of specialization, are the secrets of the superb craftsmanship found in Japanese crafts. Just as in eighteenth-century Paris or London superb furniture was made by each craftsman devoting his whole working-life only to, say, carving the knees of chairs, so in Kyoto today, men still devote a long working-life only to folding fans or forging knives and do it supremely well, producing perfect fans and perfect knives. But today, in most crafts, the average age of the workmen is high. In many of them, for both social and economic reasons, it may be difficult to find 'tomorrow's' apprentices.

Crafts, by and large, are the artefacts of social activity, and Japanese traditional crafts, apart from any aesthetic qualities, can teach us a great deal about the Japanese way of life. Both the making and the use of the objects described in this book touch on various sides of Japanese life and, all too briefly, an attempt has been made to show how they illustrate attitudes and elements of daily life. For example, in *tatami*, the reed floor mats, there are elements of space, traditionalism, frugality and cleanliness. In *furoshiki*, the carrying cloth, there is also space and frugality, together with ingenuity. In this way every craft object in this book can help in an understanding of Japan, for though the qualities they represent are traditional qualities, these have lived on and given strength to modern life just as the objects themselves have remained in use. And if such a commentary encourages further interest and a search for more specialized books, of which there are now many, in areas of particular interest, that was a major purpose of this book.

Because the structure of Japanese society is so complex and so unusual, hardly any topic can be fairly dealt with in a few lines. Japan is not to be understood in a few weeks or even a few years. Living in Japan as I do, one soon learns the difficulty of forming lasting and viable opinions. Almost hourly, new experiences cause another revision. Trying to understand Japan often seems like trying to make sculpture with dry sand. At the very moment when one's hands begin to feel a shape, they are empty again.

It is not impossible to understand the Japanese. We are all similar, but each society structures its members from birth to obey the laws and fulfil the needs of that society. The Japanese are perhaps more heavily structured than any other nation, because of the very special needs of a society with a huge population but no natural resources and an acute lack of space. One is more aware of social structuring, both the Japanese and one's own, in Japan than anywhere else because at every step it is so evident. I went to congratulate some old friends on the birth of their first grandchild. When I entered the room the grandmother was holding the week-old baby, and as I bowed I saw her hand slip behind the baby's head gently pushing it forward in a tiny bow. No doubt in a year or two the bow would become a reflex action. That is a first step in structuring in Japan, a process that tones down individuality, instils modesty, fosters a group identity and does everything possible to eradicate the causes of friction in the human character.

If asked for any shortcuts to understanding Japan, I would advise looking at Japanese life in these terms which largely account for Japan's remarkable difference. The extent of the difference is epitomized in the fact that literally hundreds of things from craftsmen's tools to electric light switches work in exactly the opposite way to those in the Western world. Accept and recognize an almost total difference in everything and you have taken the first step in understanding Japan. But the differences are so enormous that they are hard to comprehend or accept and, even after years of firsthand experience of Japan, one must frequently remind oneself of the unique nature of Japanese society.

Finally, one must ask how long these traditional crafts, and more important, the qualities of life and character they represent, will survive? In that question lies much of the future of Japan and it is impossible to answer. Conservatism is enormously strong in Japan and considering the general movement of the world in the last twenty-five years Japan has changed remarkably little. There are signs of change, with less discipline among young people, growing juvenile delinquency, the probability that 'economic miracles' are over and other problems springing basically from the introduction of Western materialism. But it would be unwise to read too much into these things. Japanese society has an incredible resilience, and an incredible capacity for absorbing and smothering alien elements. Each year one sees how the 'company system' re-educates and tames thousands of undisciplined university graduates, mainly because the establishment holds the only key to lifelong security.

There is much in Japanese life and society that almost inevitably the foreigner will find frustrating, difficult, even unpleasant. But in making criticisms one should remember two principles. First, while something might not work in the West, it works well in Japan, and by and large the Japanese are a contented society. Secondly, before criticizing any Japanese practice, suggest a viable alternative. You will probably remain silent.

A few words about the practical side of this book. During the years I worked at West Dean College in Sussex, England, one of the few institutions anywhere wholly devoted to teaching crafts, I worked with craftsmen and women and craft teachers from all over the world. Despite the fact that during the first six years of the college we taught over one hundred and fifty different crafts, I noticed that both teachers and students were always searching for new ones. I hope this book will provide fresh opportunities for some of them.

The craft descriptions and brief practical notes are no more than a guide, but I know from experience that good craftsmen in one field have an aptitude for moving successfully into another area given the minimum necessary guidance. I would reemphasize to interested craftsmen that there is now a large number of more specialized books available and that, more and more, in the larger cities of the world, Japanese craft materials are becoming available or can be specially ordered from enterprising shops. Obviously such things as the floor mats, knives and umbrellas offer insurmountable problems, but I think the other eleven crafts offer ideas and inspiration for experiment, as each note suggests. I would like to think that many craftsmen will extract as much pleasure from attempting these crafts as we did from studying them.

By coincidence, I am writing this introduction almost exactly fifteen years since I first came to Japan. I think that within a few hours of stepping off the aeroplane in Tokyo I had fallen in love with Japan. Time has slowly injected some reality into my affections – and, from time to time, drops of cynicism, frustration and fury – but it still remains an affair of the heart. Meeting such a wide range of Japanese craftsmen and studying their work was not only a deeply interesting experience but yet again left me admiring the qualities of these men and women, ordinary yet extraordinary people who represent the heart of the Japanese nation.

Throughout the book Japanese names are given in the Western order, personal name first, family name last. The '-san' after Japanese names is the Japanese for Mr, Mrs or Miss.

疊句篇

Home
Life

1

Floor Mats
Tatami

In Japan few sights are more pleasing than the great expanses of *tatami*, their cool, tightly-textured surface stretching evenly across the great empty rooms of Kyoto temples and palaces, giving the traditional Japanese interior a quiet beauty and emphasizing the subtle qualities of space, of emptiness. *Tatami* is the heart of the traditional Japanese home. Nothing is more evocative of Japan than that special fragrance of *tatami* in the humid air of the rainy season. More and more, carpets are replacing *tatami* in modern Japanese homes, along with all the clutter of Western furniture. But most Japanese, even in a small apartment, like to keep one *tatami* room.

The whole traditional way of life belongs on the *tatami*, for that life was evolved to be lived on the floor and enjoyed from it: sitting on *tatami*; admiring a scroll-painting from the *tatami*; and spreading one's bedding on the clean *tatami*. Its woven surface is a delight to the eye, its texture a pleasure to the touch. And recently, scientists have suggested that *tatami* significantly restores oxygen to the air of the room. Without doubt the intricate craft of the *tatami*-maker will survive for a long time to come.

Tatami of one form or another date far back in Japanese history. Reed mats are mentioned as early as AD 712 but these seem to have been thin as a rug. Thick *tatami* mats, of various sizes, appeared early in the Heian period but, until the sixteenth century, did not cover the whole floor. Early portraits show emperors and the nobility seated on one mat as a kind of throne and there is evidence that both the size of the mat and the colour and style of its binding were in strict accord with a person's status. A fourteenth-century book gives some examples, such as a pattern of large clouds and chrysanthemums being suitable for princes and ministers, and yellow being an inferior colour to purple. About the middle of the sixteenth century the wealthy began to cover the entire floor with *tatami* mats and in 1622 the Shogun ordered nine thousand *tatami* mats for his castle. During the eighteenth and nineteenth centuries the use of *tatami* became more commonplace and it became the practice to describe accommodation in terms of eight-mat rooms, four-and-a-half-mat rooms, and so on. The mat became the basic unit of Japanese architecture and, in a sense, of Japanese life.

The method of constructing a *tatami* mat has changed little since they were first used in Japan. Its appearance stretched on the floor leads to a common misconception among foreigners that it is a thin mat of woven rice straw. In fact, the whole mat is bulky and heavy if lifted, its foundation a pad of compressed rice straw, about 5 cm (1·9 in.) thick, which is covered with a stretched mat of woven *igusa* reeds, the long edges of the whole mat bound with plain or patterned cotton or nylon binding. Originally all made by hand, the pad (*toko*), the woven mat (*tatami-omote*) and the binding (*fushi*) are now usually made by machine. The rice-straw pads are made wherever rice is grown, and they are also now imported from Taiwan and Korea. The *igusa* reeds are specially cultivated in Kyushu and around Okayama, and are machine-woven in the same areas. It is an extremely skilled job to weave them by hand. Even when woven by machine, they come in different qualities, the best with a finer texture and patterning. The bindings are mainly of plain or patterned cotton but sometimes of nylon and leather. The width, colouring and pattern used will depend on where the *tatami* is placed.

Today there are three standard sizes of *tatami*. The largest mat, of the Kansai area around Osaka and Kyoto, measures 192 by 96 cm (75·5 × 37·7 in.), the Tokyo size 176 by 88 cm (69·2 × 34·6 in.), and a modern 'apartment' size only 170 by 85 cm (66·9 × 33·4 in.). In the ordinary Japanese house, rooms hold between three and ten mats, but can be of unlimited size. In the larger rooms of Japanese temples, palaces and castles, there may be one hundred mats or more in one room. The mats fit tightly together, bedded on a hard surface and surrounded by a wooden moulding. The bindings form continuous lines where two mats meet. For rooms of every mat-size there are traditional patterns for laying out the mats. At the entrance to a room the first mats must be laid lengthwise as that way the line of the weaving offers the greatest resistance against wear. Needless to say, no form of footwear, not even the softest slippers, must ever be worn on *tatami*.

There is one interesting exception to the above. There is a special, softer kind of *tatami* made for such sports as judo, and formerly for the floors of kimono shops, maybe because the soft surface would not catch the trailing silk. These mats, on the same rice-straw base, are made of a thick reed, split before weaving, which comes from Aoshima island, near Okinawa. The mats for the kimono shop were bound with soft leather, but the judo-mats were left unbound and the mat was tucked securely beneath the *toko*.

As the basic unit in Japanese architectural design, and to some extent in social organization, the *tatami*, roughly two metres by one, represents the living and sleeping space of one Japanese, and sharply reminds us that the most precious commodity in Japan is space. Japan has a population of about 115,000,000 people, and a country of about the size of California of which at least three-quarters of the land surface is mountainous. The acute lack of space has had the deepest effect on every aspect of Japanese life, particularly with the growing urbanization of the last three hundred years.

It is perhaps a risky theory to propound but, whenever I find myself confronted with anything I do not understand in Japan, I first examine the problem in terms of 'lack of space'. The whole of Japanese social behaviour is better understood in these terms, where a society almost without physical privacy has, through attitudes and etiquette, provided an intangible privacy. This partly explains why Japanese do not shake hands, why Japanese are able to ignore what they do not wish to see or hear, the

1 The heavy pad of compressed rice straw

tolerance of society to drunkenness and what are called 'matters below the navel', a seeming lack of neighbourliness and a thousand other ways so strange to the Westerner. In our small Kyoto kitchen, I remember a Japanese friend once saying to me, while I stirred a pot with Western abandon: 'Your movements are too vivid.' It was really her way of saying: 'You are taking up more space than your allotted one mat'!

Making a Floor Mat

All around the backstreets of Kyoto are small *tatami* workshops, seldom employing more than one or two craftsmen. Hiroshi Kubo-san works by himself in a tiny workshop which he set up in 1967 having trained for three years under an experienced craftsman. He can make about six standard mats a day but he offers a range of qualities which vary as much in price as from 10,000 yen to some 22,500 yen a mat. Normally he works about eight hours a day, but in the busy seasons before New Year and when the students move into new lodgings in March, he works around the clock. Kubo-san not only showed us the full process of making a mat but gave us a great deal of background information. For all the various qualities and sizes of mat the basic craft process is the same as in the making of a standard Kansai mat described here.

All *tatami* are made up of three components: the heavy, chopped-straw pad, the woven reed mat which covers it, and the cotton or nylon binding down the two long sides. Putting these together is quite a complicated process. Everything used to be made by hand but today machinery is used at every stage and some modern materials have crept in. Kubo-san thought it would now be difficult to get *tatami* made entirely by hand and that the cost would be enormous. In position on the floor the *tatami* looks like a delicate, lightweight woven mat. In fact, with its straw pad, it averages a weight of about 25 to 30 kg (55–66 lb).

When a householder wants new *tatami* for a room, the first step is for Kubo-san to visit the house and check the measurements of the room. Exact fitting is essential. Back in the workshop, Kubo-san first takes the base of the mat, the heavy chopped rice-straw pad which he buys ready-made from the nearby Shiga prefecture. In the old days these pads or *toko* were made by hand as winter work for the farmer's family. This is extremely skilled and some are still made by hand, but mostly they are now made by a machine first invented about one hundred years ago by a member of the Toyota family. The compressed chopped straw is held together by interwoven string. The best pads are all straw but a cheaper version now sandwiches a layer of expanded polystyrene between two layers of straw. Formerly the

2 Plastic moulding and reeds strengthen the ends of the pad

3 The mat is stretched over the pad and tightened

base of the pad was covered with a woven straw mat but today this is replaced with a plastic sheet which is firmly stitched to the pad by machine. The finished pad, though slightly flexible, is extremely strong and solid. A well-made pad will last for twenty to thirty years, but the reed mat must be replaced about every five years.

The straw pads are delivered slightly larger than needed and must be trimmed to the correct size. In the first stage, using a large aluminium T-square, Kubo-san trims only the ends with a special knife. Now he must begin to fit the reed mat to the pad. Again the mats are delivered from their makers a little oversize leaving the *tatami*-maker a slight margin in getting the final exact fit. The correct width of the mat is measured with bamboo rulers and is marked on only one side by cutting a few centimetres at three points: at either end and in the middle. The mats are delivered folded and to remove these folds the mat is laid out on the straw pad and the creases dampened with water (Kubo-san spits on them after taking a long swig of water from a bottle). When the water dries the creases vanish.

Now the mat is pinned to the pad. First, a right-angled length of plastic moulding is laid along the top of both ends of the pad and some reeds are laid along the upper edge of this plastic edging. Then the mat is pinned down at each end with nine long pins or small spikes, which are put in just below the plastic edging. The outer pins are placed first; then the centre pin; then three between the outer and centre pin; and the three remaining between the other centre and outer pin – this to make certain that the mat is pinned centrally and completely evenly. The pinning is done at both ends.

Before it can be stitched to the pad, the mat must now be tightened. This is done by placing a batten of wood under one end of the pad which bends the pad very slightly. Then, by removing the pins in the right order, one by one from left to right, the mat is tightened. Water is also sprayed over the

4 The sewing machine sews down the binding

5 The thickness is adjusted by putting reeds under the binding

6 The binding is sewn to the pad by hand

7 The hand-stitching is tightened with a steel hook

mat during this process which tightens the mat as it dries. Careful attention must be given to the parallel lines in the woven pattern of the reeds as these show if the mat is being overstretched anywhere which would make it thinner at that point. It is important to keep an even thickness so that in use the mat will wear evenly. When the mat is tightened correctly, the edges of the mat are trimmed off with a knife and rule.

Next the whole *tatami* is turned over and the thickness around all its edges measured with a special U-shaped wooden gauge called a *buatari*. Often the *tatami* is thicker in the middle, in which case rushes are added along the edge between the mat and the pad to get an equal thickness all over. The mat-ends are now stitched to the pad using a 10 to 12 cm (3·9–4·7 in.) steel needle and yellow nylon thread. The needle only lasts about three months. It is pushed through the *tatami* by the palm of the hand which is covered by a triangular leather pad strapped to the hand. Today, in cheap *tatami*, the stitching is often replaced by large metal staples. When the stitching is complete, it is pulled tight with a metal hook and the slack taken up and tied. Both ends of the *tatami* are stitched in this way.

Stitching the long sides of the *tatami* with the cloth binding (*fuchi*), is now done, usually with a large, specially-designed sewing machine. First the *tatami* is turned over again so that the reed mat is uppermost. The length of cotton binding is then laid face downwards along the edge of the *tatami*, the outer edge of the binding about 2 cm (0·8 in.) from the edge of the *tatami*. Then a narrower strip of strong paper is laid over the cotton binding, the edge of the paper along the outer edge of the binding. Later, when the binding is turned over the edge of the *tatami*, this paper forms an inner lining. Now a steel rail is laid parallel to the pinned binding and paper along the whole length of the *tatami*, and the sewing machine runs along this rail, stitching the binding along the full length of the *tatami*. The process is repeated on both sides.

If the binding is stitched by hand, before the *tatami* is turned upwards the craftsman goes down each side of the pad removing the woven string where his stitching will go and also softening the pad by hammering it along the line where he will stitch. He then turns the *tatami* upwards, places the binding and paper strip in the same way, and stitches them by hand with the yellow nylon thread and a smaller steel needle about 8 to 10 cm (3·1–3·9 in.) long. Afterwards, from the bottom side, the stitching is pulled tight with the metal hook and the slack secured. Hand-stitching takes about ten times as long as machine-stitching and is not necessarily stronger. After the stitching is finished, the edges of the pad are finally trimmed to the exact size with a knife or an electric hand-saw.

Now the binding, with its paper lining, is turned over the edges of the *tatami*. First a line is drawn along the paper lightly with a knife to make the

5

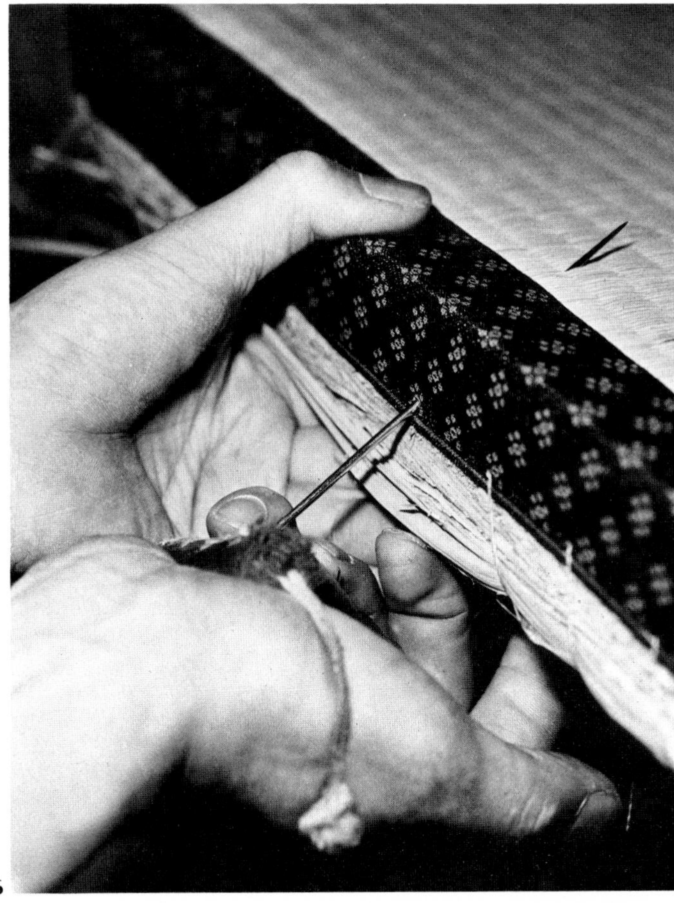
6

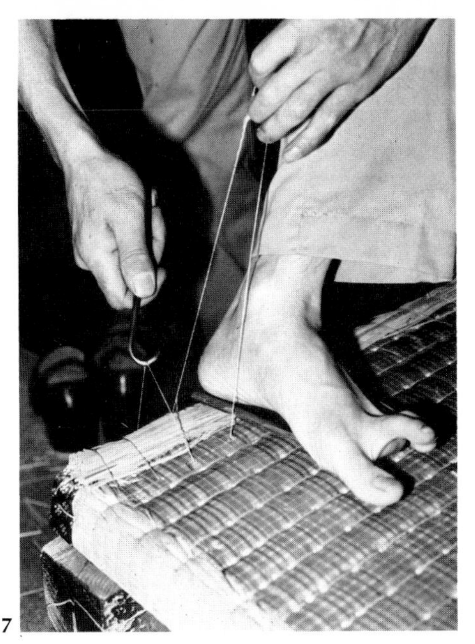
7

paper and binding fold over neatly at the correct place. The cloth and paper are folded and stretched tightly over the *tatami*, revealing the upper side and correct pattern of the binding which now covers about 3 cm (1·2 in.) of the upper edge, and the side of the *tatami*. The binding is now stitched to the straw pad, either by hand or by machine. In both cases, first the end of the binding is stitched down, and after that it is stitched along the full length on both sides. Again the thickness can be adjusted by inserting a few reeds under the binding before stitching, which also has the effect of tightening the stitching. If the binding is hand-stitched, the hook must be used to give a final tightening to the stitches. The binding is never put on the ends of the *tatami*. The stretched mat gives sufficient strength to the ends, and the layout of the mats in a room, whatever its size, depends for its effect on the parallel lines of the side bindings, the unbound abutting ends giving a continuous effect of woven matting.

It can be seen from this description that there are several variations which are possible in making a *tatami*, and in these lie the variations in quality and in price.

2

Kitchen Knives
Hōcho

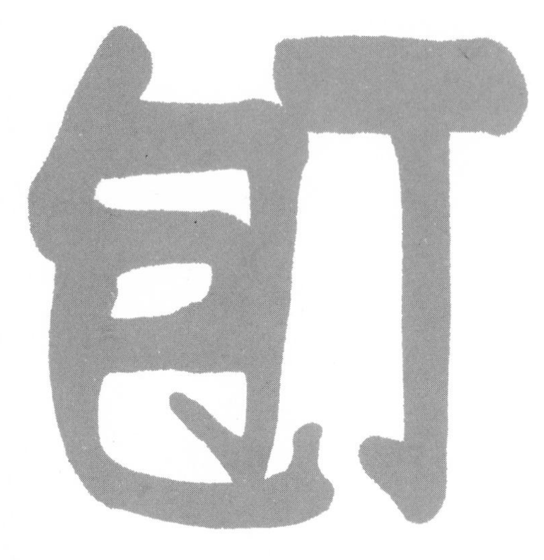

In the glittering shopping streets and arcades of central Kyoto, nothing is more spectacular than the small shops selling traditional kitchen knives. The walls are lined with row upon row of glistening blades ranged in an amazing variety of shapes and sizes. Western connoisseurs have long admired the immaculate beauty of the samurai sword. Although of less heroic purpose, the traditional Japanese kitchen knife offers an almost equal aesthetic pleasure and should command something of the same respect. It is the happiest marriage of form and function; a perfect instrument, perfectly designed and perfectly made. And the essence of its beauty lies in its streamlined simplicity.

The Japanese have been master sword-makers for centuries, and related skills have been evolved and refined to serve the needs of daily life in every kitchen in Japan. Even today, when both Japanese and foreign modern stainless steel knives are readily available, there can be few Japanese housewives who do not still use traditional *hōcho*, while for the Japanese professional cook any other form of knife would be unthinkable. The use of traditional knives is inseparably linked to the preparation of traditional dishes, which bodes well for the future of this fine craft.

These traditional knives, together with carpenters' tools and special types of scissors for such activities as flower arranging, are made in small factories in many places in Japan, even in the heart of cosmopolitan Tokyo. We made this study with the help of an old and most famous Kyoto firm, Kikuichi Monji, who were exceptionally generous in the help they gave us. The firm is said to have been founded in Kyoto seven hundred years ago, and has a factory three hundred and fifty years old. A former Emperor granted the firm the right to put the Imperial symbol of the chrysanthemum on their knives. This unusual honour is reflected in the firm's name which literally means 'the character of one chrysanthemum' (*kiku*).

They now have two shops in the centre of Kyoto. The factory, which used to be nearby, was moved to the southern suburbs of the city in 1974 because of pollution problems. They do not make everything they sell as their stock is enormous. Their catalogue is an encyclopedia of Japanese cutlery and specialist tools: knives, cooking implements, woodworking and textile-makers' tools, a variety of scissors, and a range of pruning and gardening implements. For anyone who loves fine tools, the shops of Kikuichi Monji are Aladdin's caves, and a sore temptation to the purse.

Japanese knives are unique in two ways: their manufacture and their incredible specialization. First, the Japanese knife blade is made by 'sandwiching' hard steel between soft iron, the slightly projecting line of hard steel providing the cutting edge. The process is described in detail in the craft section of this chapter. Extreme sharpness is vital for these knives, and this way of making the blade makes sharpening easier and more effective. All Japanese knives and tools are sharpened on a wet stone; oil stones are not used. Because the relationship between the iron and the steel differs slightly in different types of knife, each knife must be sharpened in the correct way. For example, a *sushi* knife, where the steel core is more exposed on one side than the other, must be sharpened seven times on one side to only three on the other. With vegetable knives, where the steel core is in the centre of the iron, the knife is sharpened five times on each side. Since the finest kitchen knives can cost 25,000 yen or more, it is senseless to buy a traditional knife unless one knows how to sharpen it. Because of their peculiar structure they need frequent sharpening and also for that reason they are easily ruined.

The weight and balance of these knives is also of great importance. Professional cooks tend to use heavier knives, which by sheer weight and extreme sharpness do most of the work with the minimum of pressure and effort. This is important since in traditional Japanese cooking there is a vast amount of cutting and fine slicing which must be done with speed and accuracy. The knife handles, which must be finely balanced with the blades, are usually made of a white wood from the *Ho* tree. The collar joining the handle and the blade is made of African buffalo horn on expensive knives, and stainless steel on cheaper knives.

Japanese knives are also unique in their amazing degree of specialization. If ever the saying, 'the right tool for the right job', could be applied anywhere, it could certainly be applied in the Japanese kitchen, be it in the home or the restaurant. Monji's catalogue lists ninety-one different types of kitchen knife, ranging from a 'watermelon-cutting knife' through to a double-handled knife for cutting the special rice cakes served at the New Year. Their list could easily be lengthened by adding special regional knives developed by craftsmen for the preparation of local specialities.

Fish has long played a major part in Japanese cooking, and the special problems of preparing, and particularly boning, certain types of fish has resulted in special knives shaped to deal with a particular fish. Of the kitchen knives listed by Kikuichi Monji, thirty-one are for fish, with special knives for preparing bonito, tunny, eel, sea-eel, shell fish, horse-mackerel and globefish, quite apart from many more general-purpose fish knives. There are knives for chicken, for 'hens' bowels', bread, cake, meat, Chinese cooking, cleaving, paring, butchering and, of course, a variety for vegetables.

In Japanese cooking, the appearance and general presentation of traditional dishes can on occasion be of greater importance than the taste. Because of this the cutting and slicing of ingredients follow set rules and styles. Each vegetable must be sliced in the correct way and at the correct angle, and the right cut will only be achieved with the right knife, properly sharpened. Most particularly, the whole art of serving raw fish depends on the right knives.

The speed and dexterity of Japanese cooks is breathtaking, particularly in their slicing and chopping. Like the Japanese carpenter with his tools, the Japanese cook makes the cut on the 'pull' rather than, in the Western way, on the 'push'. The implement is under greater control while being pulled as anyone will appreciate who has learned to use a Japanese saw. This control gives the Japanese cook a remarkable accuracy, again helped by the extreme sharpness of his knife. When it comes to boning some of the fish such as the *hamo* eel so popular in Kyoto, the tiny bones would defeat all but the specially designed knife, and in Japanese cooking not one single bone must be left.

This may all be part of a traditional ritual, yet just the look of these beautifully made knives commands a certain respect. Just as one admires the flashing swordplay of the samuari warrior, so, seated at the bar of a small Japanese restaurant, one's pleasure of the meal is enhanced by admiring the cooks' dexterity with their knives and the sense of devotion, almost dependence, with which they sharpen them. Even after years in Japan, I can never pass a good knife shop without gazing reverently in.

Making a Kitchen Knife

From the outside the knife factory was a nondescript building, and inside it was gloomy and noisy, with about seven craftsmen working among the glowing furnaces and the unceasing throb of power hammers. The dirt and seeming disorder were in marked contrast to the glistening order of the knife shops in central Kyoto. But it was here, in these drab surroundings, that the beautiful, gleaming traditional knives were forged, using the unique Japanese method of bonding soft iron around a core of hard steel by a process that has changed little in a hundred years, except for the introduction of electrically-driven power-hammers and grinding-wheels.

The soft iron and the high carbon steel used to make the knives are brought from Osaka in long strips suitable for the bonding process. These metals are heated in small brick furnaces fuelled with coke and pinewood. They can reach a temperature of about 1200°C. The craftsman starts by heating a narrow strip of iron in the furnace. When it is sufficiently hot, he cuts a long narrow slot down the centre of the iron bar with a carbon steel chisel. To assist the bonding a special sand is sprinkled in this slot, after which a suitably-sized strip of high carbon steel is inserted in the slot, sandwiched by the soft iron. The whole strip is now put back in the furnace and heated for about two minutes to 750°C.

8

8 A slot is cut down the centre of the iron bar with a chisel

9 The carbon steel is sandwiched in the iron bar

9

10

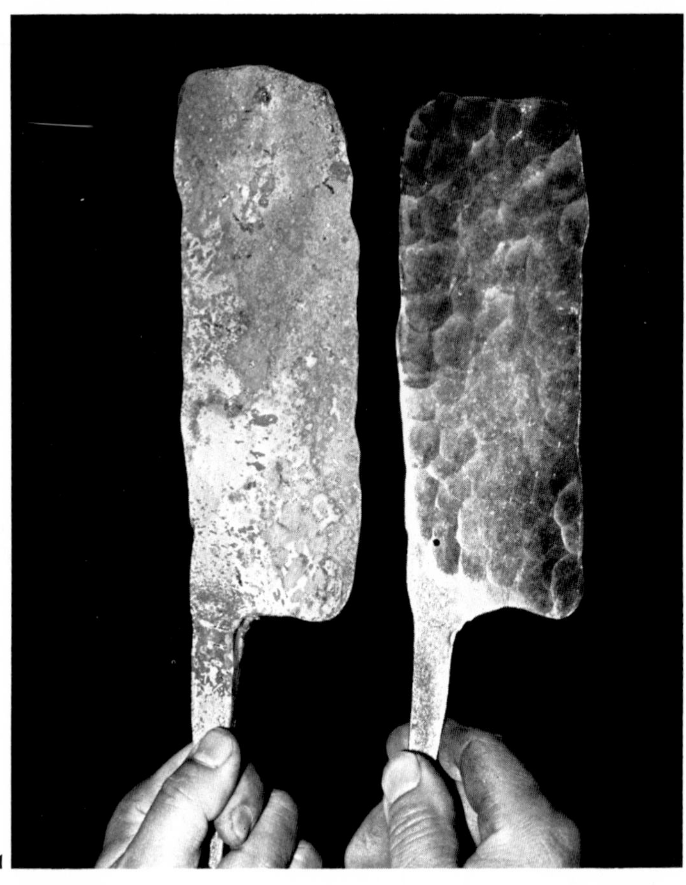

11

10 Rough blades waiting to be heated in the furnace

11 The blade with the tang formed at one end

The strip is now malleable enough to be beaten out by a power-hammer into the rough shape of the knife blade. This pounding also increases the bonding between the iron and the central core of steel. Only the front part of the strip is shaped and, when the rough form of the blade has been beaten out, this is cut off with a chisel and hammer. This roughly-shaped blade is again heated in the furnace, and a small notch made a quarter of the way along the top edge. This split in the metal allows the hammer to form the back of the blade into the tang, that spiked part of the blade which will fit into the knife handle. Forming this tang bends the blade, so once again it must be heated and straightened, this hammering furthering the shaping and thinning of the metal.

Oxidization caused by impurities in the coke furnace will have dulled the surface of the blade and this must now be removed. When the blade has cooled, it is hammered over a steel block with a concave surface. As the blade bends and vibrates under the hammering that forces it down into the hollow of the block, the layers of oxidization flake off leaving the blade with a dull metallic lustre which can now be brought to a high polish. The blade is again straightened and hammered further, the first step in smoothing and

12 Oxidization is cleared by hammering the blade on a concave block

polishing the surface of the metal. Next, with a large and heavy stamping machine, the rough blade is cut to its proper shape. The blade is now ready for the final stages of tempering, grinding and polishing.

The first edge is given to the blade with a large and fairly coarse grinding-wheel. It is then further sharpened on a rather less coarse stone. Now the whole blade, having first been washed and dried, is covered with a paste made of soil and charcoal powder. It is then heated and plunged into cold water. This process tempers and hardens the blade, and particularly the steel core. It is the correct tempering of the cutting edge that will enable it to achieve the sharpness required, not far short of a razor. The blade is heated once again and then left to cool naturally. The shape of the blade is checked at each stage and a special hammer is used to beat out every imperfection.

With some knives, at this stage an iron-filing spray gun is used to roughen the surface of the soft iron along the line of the blade where it meets the hard steel cutting edge. This is a decorative effect, to highlight and contrast the two metals used in making the blade. All knives of any quality are stamped with the maker's name on the blade.

The blade is now dipped in some anti-corrosive agent for a period, then dried and cleaned. It is then given the final sharpening and polishing, using a rough, medium and fine stone, always with water, the final grinding putting a razor-sharp edge on the hard steel. After final cleaning, the blades are packed and sent to another workshop to be fitted to their wooden handles before delivery to the shops.

13 The blade cut to the correct shape. The surplus metal has been trimmed away by the stamping machine

13

14 The blade is again straightened with a power-hammer

15 One of the stages of grinding and polishing the blade

14

15

There is a kind of miracle in the way this glistening blade emerges from the dirt and noise and clumsy machinery of the knife factory. The laborious processes of heating, hammering and grinding tend to obscure the extremely delicate skill of the craftsmen whose judgment must be as sharp and precise as the magnificent knives they fashion.

Practical Note

Obviously the making of traditional Japanese knives is not something for the amateur craftsmen. Despite that, I would like to make two practical points. First, these knives tend to be extremely expensive, so do not waste your money buying one unless you are positive you know the correct way to sharpen it. But for those who know, or who can be bothered to learn, I warmly recommend all Japanese knives and tools to Western craftsmen – if you can get hold of them. A few years ago some of my woodworking students were given a demonstration of Japanese woodworking tools. Because these tend to look primitive, they began by being both sceptical and scornful. However, by the end of the demonstration, every student was asking me if I would buy him some tools when I was next visiting Japan.

3

Brooms
Hōki

In the centre of Kyoto where the Sanjo bridge crosses the Kamogawa river stands a tall stone which marks the end of the old road between Tokyo and Kyoto. A few yards to the west is an open-fronted, cavernous shop, where in perpetual gloom stand, hang and lie a remarkable assortment of traditional Japanese household and craft brushes and brooms. Apart from the wide selection of ordinary brooms, there are special brushes and brooms for getting dust out of drawers, brushing false teeth, cleaning a radish grater, brushing iron kettles, garden brooms for sweeping moss, and a variety of brushes for different crafts. The smaller brushes lie in trays in front of the shop. The old-fashioned interior is crammed with larger brushes and brooms, a forest of bamboo handles. There are few traditional shops now left in Kyoto with more atmosphere.

This famous shop was started by the Naitō family two hundred years ago, and today is owned by Daiji Naitō-san. Sadly, however, the demand for traditional brushes and brooms has drastically declined since the Second World War. Cheap, machine-made brooms, together with the growing use of vacuum cleaners, has eroded the Naitōs' market. Their stock has shrunk and they now only sell ten per cent of what they sold twenty-five years ago. Naitō-san's father was a broom-maker but there seemed no future in the craft for his son. His mother now runs the shop, while he works for a trading company in Osaka. With this situation and few craftsmen left, the craft of Kyoto broom-making may well vanish before long.

The main feature of many of these traditional brushes and brooms is that they are made of the soft but extremely hard-wearing fibre peeled from the trunk of the hemp palm, a semi-tropical tree which grows in many parts of Japan. However, some are made of other materials. Small brushes are made of duck and pigeon feathers for dusting inside the house. Brushes made of rice straw are used for cleaning kitchen ranges, and many larger brooms are made of millet. There is a special garden broom made of ferns from the South Seas, and a variety of garden rakes, essential in the care of moss, are made of bamboo. The various types of broom, with or without long and short bamboo handles, are bound together with strong cotton thread and thin copper wires and copper rings. The craft section describes the process at its most complicated. Just about the only kinds of brushes not sold in the Naitōs' shop are those for writing and painting. This is a separate craft with its own special shops, described in Chapter Eight.

In the past the Japanese had a special liking for 'the right tool for the right job', and it was to provide for all the needs of Japanese domestic life that they evolved such an exceptionally wide range of brushes and brooms. The rather fragile construction of a Japanese house, with *tatami* woven reed-matting covering all the floors and the delicate *shōji* sliding doors, a wooden lattice 'glazed' with thin paper, created special cleaning problems. All over the world the vacuum cleaner has replaced the range of brooms and brushes that used to be found everywhere, but Japanese vacuum cleaners still have a special switch which enables them to clean the *tatami*.

Two personal experiences of such Japanese problems linger in my mind. I once lived for a few days as a 'novice' in a large Zen monastery of the Soto sect. I was given a small Japanese-style room which was all *tatami* and papered *shōji*. I was told that after attending the early morning service, my next duty, between 5 and 6 o'clock, would be to clean my room until every square inch shone like a mirror. Most of the few hours allowed for sleeping I lay awake worrying how one could make *tatami* and paper screens 'shine'. The *tatami* turned out to need a simple application of gentle but prolonged elbow-grease. For the *shōji*, and the tiers of dust-gathering ledges, I was given a special 'brush', a short, flexible length of bamboo fitted at one end with a number of long cloth tails, made to whip away delicately every speck of dust. I tried hard. But I shall never forget that daily look of scorn that I got from the monk in charge as he ran his finger along each 'unshining' ledge!

In very different circumstances, more recently I had charming lodgings in an old Kyoto Zen temple where I lived for a year purely as a 'layman'. Outside my rooms was a beautiful simple moss garden. Very often, around dawn, I was gently woken by the soft sound of brushing, and there was my landlady tending the moss with the care of a mother brushing her child's hair. I can still hear that early morning sound and it reminds me that all those simple-seeming pleasures and beauties of Japan are only created with enduring effort, patience and skill, be it only with a garden rake or broom.

This enormous range of Japanese brushes and brooms prompts questions about Japanese attitudes to cleanliness. Without doubt, the Japanese have the highest standards of personal cleanliness in the world. Even a Japanese hippy's gear tends to be spotlessly laundered. Shinto, the ancient and indigenous religion, rooted in strong elements of ritual purification with an emphasis on the sacredness of water, is almost certainly the source of Japan's pleasant obsession and the reverence for and delight in water, which in Japan is a gift of nature rather than something that merely comes out of the tap. Not long after the introduction of Buddhism in the sixth century, the Buddhists took over from Shinto the 'unclean' rites surrounding death and burial. Outside every Shinto shrine there is a trough with running water and ladles, where people may wash their hands and mouth, purifying themselves before entering.

Within the Japanese home some cleanliness was first based on necessity. Originally shoes were removed on entering a house to protect the *tatami*. But this sensible practice now continues even where carpets have largely replaced the reed mats. However, whereas in the past people strode about barefoot on the *tatami*, winter or summer, today the Japanese are less hardy.

Overleaf
Floor Mats
Plate 1 Standard *tatami* used in modern houses and apartments, with a plain cotton binding. (See Chapter One)

Inside the front door warm slippers await you which are only removed if you enter a *tatami* room. You will be offered a change of slippers if you enter a 'dirty' area such as the kitchen, and you will find other special slippers waiting for you just inside the lavatory. Should you think this practice complicated and fussy, think for a moment about your own carpets after you have walked the city streets or the country lanes for an hour or two!

Like anyone else, the Japanese are not wholly consistent. The appalling litter problems on the summer slopes of Mount Fuji and many other beauty spots, and the horrendous trauma of the occasional public convenience, contrast sharply and almost inexplicably with attitudes that do not allow a girl to wear the same spotless clothes two days running in case her classmates think her dirty. And in the Tokyo subway at the height of the summer, as elderly men pull up their trousers, the summer longjohns are revealed, tucked securely into the tops of their socks, both a physical and a psychological 'armour' against the dirt of the world.

It is strange that in a city that used to produce one of the finest brooms in the world, the brooms available today are among the worst. And this despite the fact that every household still needs a broom. Recently I asked my local hardware shop for a traditional Kyoto broom. It was five minutes before they understood exactly what I wanted and they then assured me that they were no longer made. They were amazed when I finally convinced them that these brooms were still available.

There are a number of Japanese superstitions concerning brooms. The god of brooms is also the god of birth, so it is considered lucky to stand a broom in the room of an expectant mother or even to stroke her stomach with it. When someone is sweeping with a broom, do not stand in their path for the flying dust can drive you mad. And, a final word of caution. Never walk over a broom or step on it. In Japan those acts may bring you a divine punishment. However, if you are suffering from an unwelcome guest, and are prepared to take the risk, then stand on your broom. It is almost certain that your guest will leave!

Making a Broom

No craftsman was kinder or more generous with his time than Yoshio Ishikawa-san, maker of traditional Kyoto brooms. His craft has suffered in the same way as the Naitōs' shop, and may well shortly disappear. Today Ishikawa-san makes his main living running a small hardware shop, and for a few hours each evening he makes brooms in a small workshop behind his store. Before the Second World War he employed seven broom-makers. He still makes a variety of brooms, some of which he sells himself, the rest

16 A finished broom

through the Naitōs and a few other shops. It takes Ishikawa-san about two hours to make the kind of broom described here, but competition from cheap brooms now makes it impossible for him to obtain a price which is a reasonable return for his labour, let alone his skill. It is not surprising that his son has no interest in continuing the broom-making business.

Ishikawa-san offered to make a Kyoto-style, long-handled broom, the most elaborate and highest-quality Japanese broom. Only he and about four other craftsmen in Kyoto still know how to make them. Ishikawa-san prepared for work wrapped in a patterned apron. He settled himself on the floor, chopping blocks, tools and materials neatly to hand. From the look of enthusiasm which brightened his keen eyes, one might have thought that he was settling down to make his first broom.

Although the materials and tools are simple, making this type of broom is complicated. It involves about forty different stages. It may help readers if they first carefully study the completed broom. In simplest terms, seven rolls of palm-hemp are attached with cotton thread, copper wire and copper rings to one end of a bamboo handle. They are held in the rigid 'fan-shape' by a lateral spike of bamboo which pierces the bamboo handle near its base. The lower part of each hemp roll is spread to form the brush head. The upper part of each roll is bound to form a 'tail' which can be securely tied to the handle and the crosspiece. This requires both skill and experience.

These brooms are made from sheets of fibrous hemp (*shuro*), which grows in overlapping layers, encircling the trunk of the hemp palm. Ishikawa-san gets his hemp from Tanba, in the neighbouring prefecture of Hyōgo, where the slightly colder climate produces stronger fibres. *Shuro* brooms have long been popular with Japanese housewives. A well-made broom has a long life and its fibres do not damage *tatami* (see Chapter One). There was a broom hanging in the workshop which Ishikawa-san's father had made thirty years ago. It showed surprising little sign of wear although in regular use.

The *shuro* is harvested each spring and autumn. At each season six sheets may be peeled off. For broom-making the sheets must be about 20 cm (7·9 in.) wide which a tree only starts to produce when ten to fifteen years old. The sheets are made into bundles and stored until required. Many traditional crafts fell victim to the Second World War; broom-making suffered when the military authorities commandeered all the *shuro* to make ropes.

Depending on the quality of the broom, up to thirty-five sheets of *shuro* can be used; one year's supply from three trees. The first stage is to make the seven rolls of *shuro*, called *tama*. Depending on their position in the 'fan', the rolls are made and bound differently from each other since certain rolls need greater strength or rigidity. Achieving these correct balances is at the heart of the craft and is what produces an efficient broom.

常信作
常信作
常信作
常信作
¥12000
¥16000
¥14000
¥4000
¥5000

Kitchen Knives
Plate 2 Fine-quality knives for cutting fish
Plate 3 A variety of knives for slicing fish and vegetables. (See Chapter Two)

17

17 The hemp is rubbed by hand to soften and separate the fibres

18 The sheets are rolled together to make a *tama*

19 The straw bundle is placed at the top end of the *tama* which is then rolled around it

20 The top end of each *tama* is bound with cotton thread. A length of wire, attached to the floor, joined to a piece of thin cord, forms a simple binding 'vice' ensuring tightness

First the sheets are dampened, and then rubbed together to soften and stretch the fibres. The softer fibres will be used on the outside and the harder ones in the centre of the roll. The hard edges of the sheets are cut off with a sharp knife and, with scissors and a bamboo measure, the sheets are trimmed to the correct length. Finally, just before rolling, the sheets are frayed lengthwise to start the separation of the fibres.

Of the seven rolls in the broom head, the middle roll and the two on the outside are made of four sheets, and the other four rolls have only two sheets – for this broom twenty sheets in all. Choosing the sheets, balancing the hard and soft fibres, and rolling the *tama* correctly, with the seams in the right place, are skills perfected by years of experience. But, as Ishikawa-san emphasized, a good broom depends on well-made *tama*. With each *tama*, a small amount of straw is folded into a short bundle and placed at the top end of the sheets. The sheets are then rolled around it, the straw making an inner wadding which helps spread the fibres into a bushy broom head.

Each *tama* is now tied with cotton thread. In all stages of binding, maximum tightness is vital to give the broom the necessary strength. This is achieved by using a simple vice (*manriki*). At Ishikawa-san's side a length of fine wire was attached to the floor with a cord and ring at his end. Binding this cord around the *tama* and pulling it tight before binding on the thread achieved a tightness impossible with the thread alone. Thus all seven *tama* are tightly bound, the thread forming a waist just over halfway up, with the narrower 'tail' above. The tail is then turned back to allow the wad of straw to be trimmed. The protrusion of the straw above where the *tama* is bound regulates the exact position of that *tama* when attached to the handle, each roll occupying a slightly different position moving out from the centre.

Now comes the second binding with copper wire and rings. The wire is fed off a simple spool. Again using his *manriki* for maximum tightness, Ishikawa-san bound the tops of the three central *tama* with copper wire about 4 cm (1·6 in.) above the thread binding. The two rolls on either side are bound with three copper rings, and the two outer *tama* with six copper rings. The copper rings are fixed by being slightly flattened with a hammer. The seven *tama* are now ready to be attached to the broom handle.

The bamboo for the handles comes from Japan's southern island, Kyushu. The lower, older wood is best for broom handles and Ishikawa-san can recognize it by the thickness of the rings along the pole's length. Having chosen a suitable length of bamboo, about 140 cm (55 in.), he cuts two V-notches on opposite sides of it, about 4 cm (1·6 in.) above the end. He then cuts a thin bamboo spike about 24 cm (9·4 in.) long which he sharpens at both ends. This spike is put through the handle and held firm in the two notches, and will be the anchoring crosspiece for all the *tama* except for the central one.

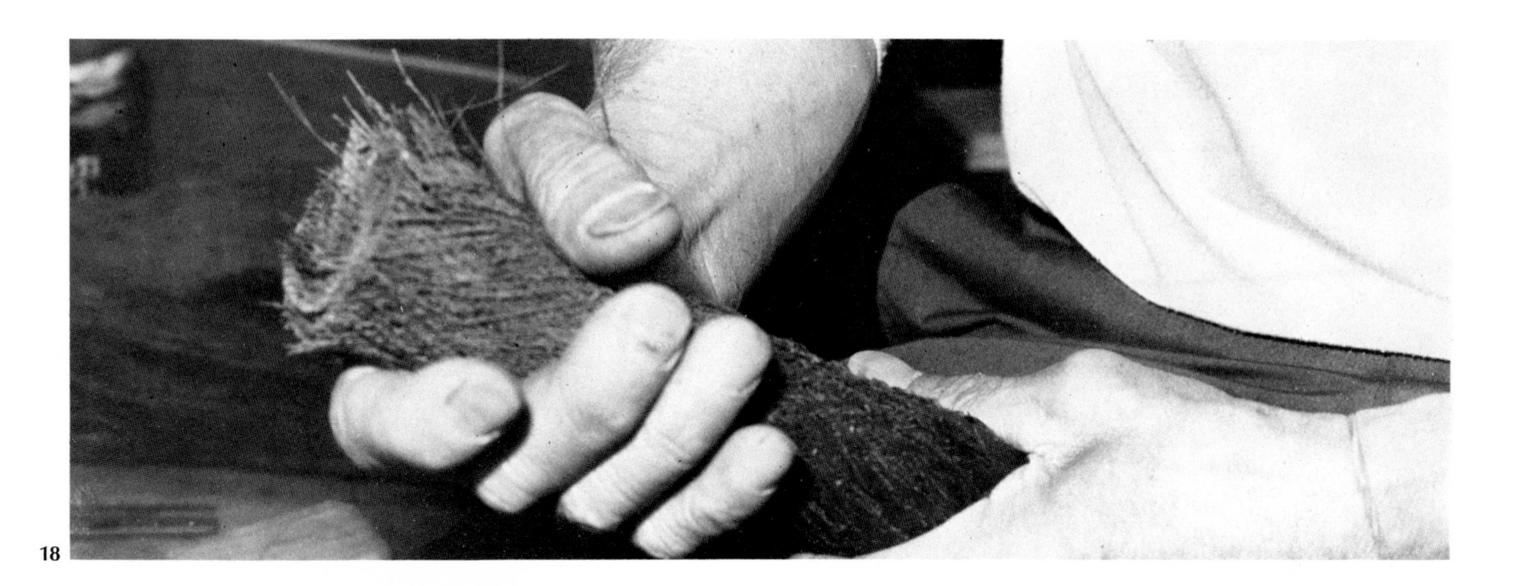

18

19

20

Folding Fans
Plate 5 A richly decorated, painted and stencilled fan

Brooms
Plate 4 The head of a Kyoto *shuro* broom. (See Chapter Three)

21 The finished copper-wire binding

22 A bundle of straw wrapped around the base of the handle

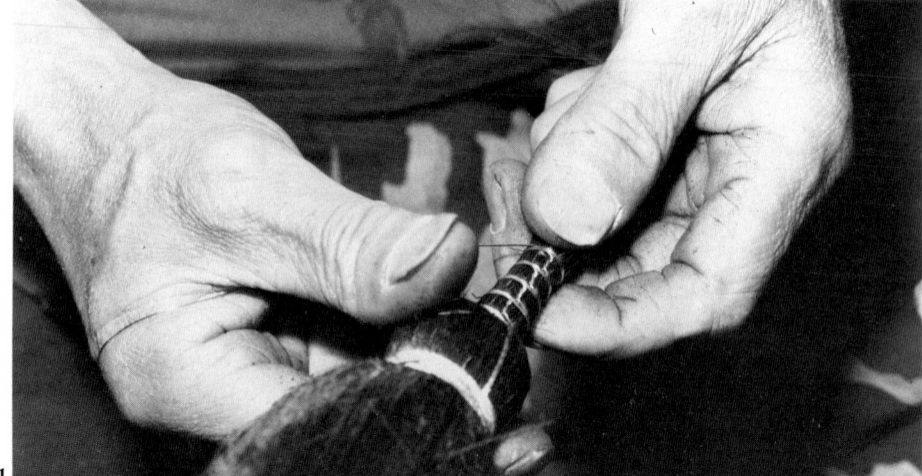

21

22

Now the seven *tama* are fitted to the handle, working from the centre outwards. First, a small bundle of straw is wrapped around the base of the handle, and the central *tama* is fitted around this bedding and bound to the handle with thread, the straw allowing the thread to bite tightly.

Now the bamboo spike is tapped through the handle until it sticks out equally on both sides. The spike also passes through the binding of the central *tama*, fixing it more firmly to the handle. Next a small hole is made through the thread bindings of the six remaining *tama* with a metal spike. In turn these *tama* are threaded by these holes on to the bamboo spike, three on each side. They are tapped firmly into position and bound to the main handle by their tails, using copper wire. When all are in position, the tails are gathered around the handle and secured with six copper rings. The rings are then tightened by hammering a slip of bamboo down between the handle and the binding.

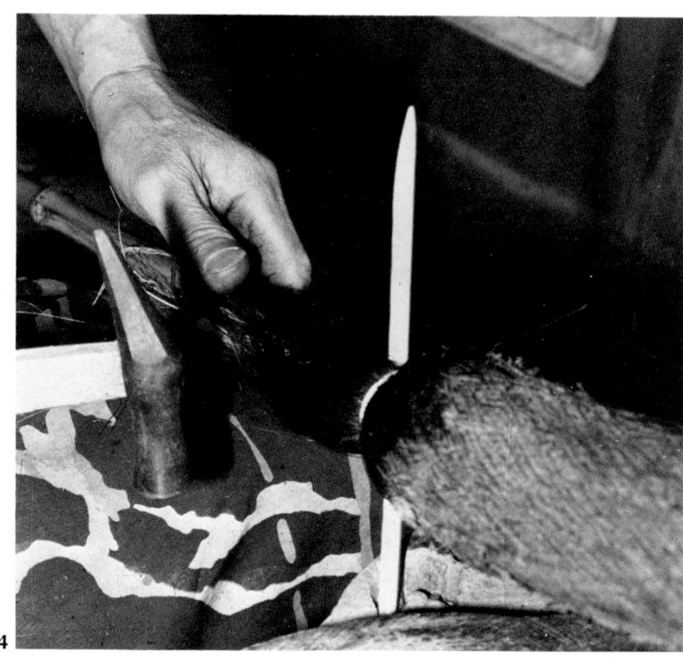

23 The first *tama* is bound on to the end of the handle. Note that the wire vice is used at every stage of binding to ensure maximum tightness

24 The bamboo spike is hammered through the handle and the binding of the first *tama*, the two notches holding the spike in position

The loose tufts now left sticking out above the six rings are turned down, and a second slip of bamboo is hammered in. Then the tufts are released, bound down with thread and copper wire to give a neat finish, and the top fringe trimmed off with a knife. The protruding ends of the bamboo spike are sawn off flush with the *tama*.

Additional support must now be given to the main body of the brush to keep it firm while sweeping, and to keep the fan spread. The brush is loosely tied together, and placed in a special wooden clamp which spreads the fibres in the correct position. With a long needle Ishikawa-san sews thread through and around the *tama*, about 3 cm (1·2 in.) below the first thread binding. To make the brush sweep efficiently, the fibres at the head are now roughly broken up by hand and afterwards combed with a crude nail-comb. Then the edge of the broom is straightened with a heavy chopping knife. Finally, a hole is drilled through the top of the broom handle and a thread loop fixed for hanging. The Kyoto *shuro* broom is now complete.

Ishikawa-san held out the finished broom, offering it as a gift. 'If you take care of it, it could last for thirty years', he said. It is an object of real, simple beauty. The soft, rich brown of the hemp contrasts so handsomely with the intricate white threads and the glowing copper rings. Its strength and rigidity are a small miracle of ingenuity and craftsmanship which often remind me of the skill in Ishikawa-san's fingers. My broom will probably last for fifty years. Partly because it was made with such care and skill. But even more because I could never use it. How could I, knowing that only too soon it will be irreplaceable?

歌麿画

Folding Fans

Plate 6 A fan with decoration in the style of a Japanese print

Plate 7 A fan with simple decoration suitable for the summer. (See Chapter Four)

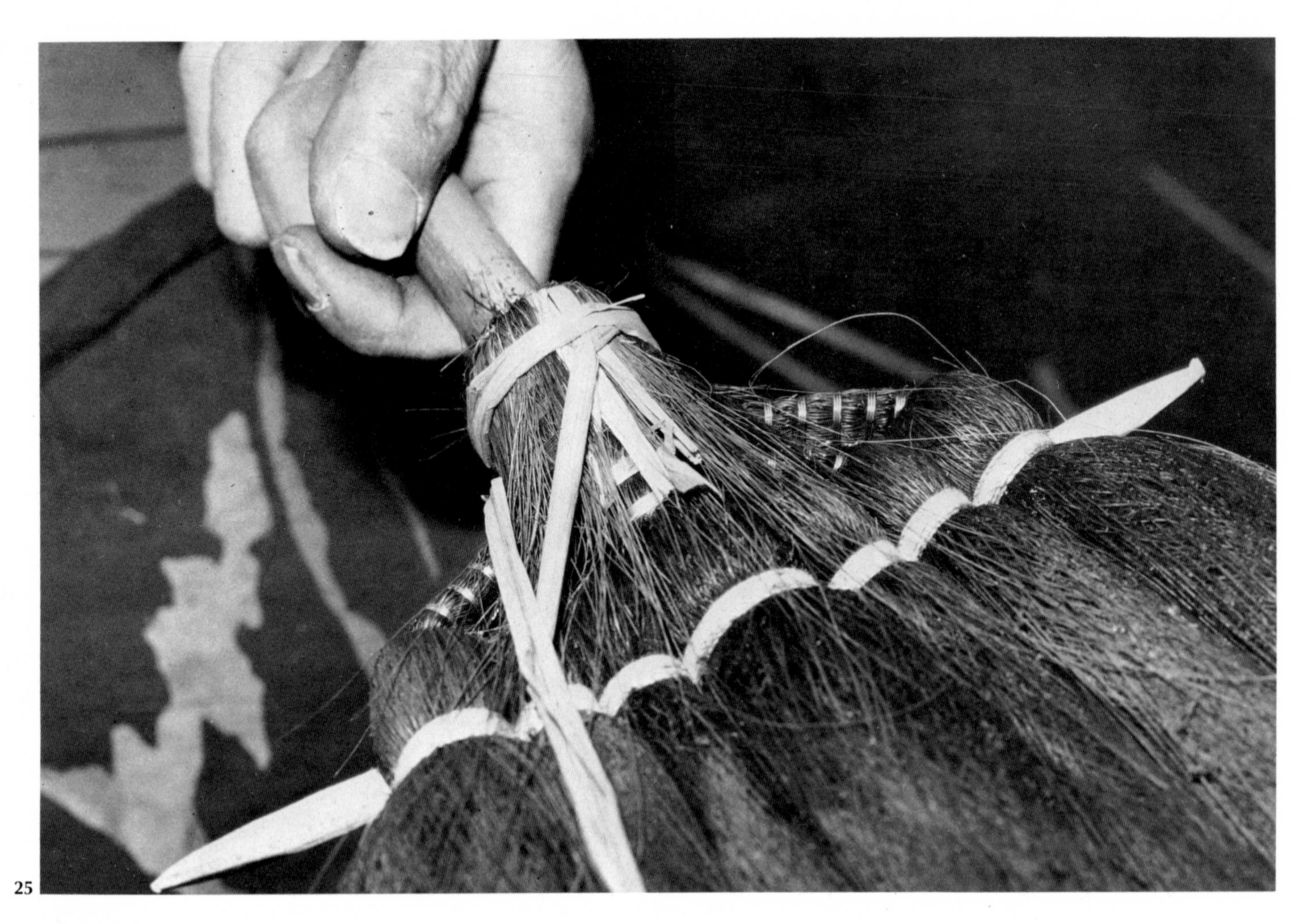

25

25 Now that all six copper rings are in position, the loose ends of the tufts are folded down and temporarily tied back

Practical Note

Obviously, the major problem is obtaining the palm-hemp, but for the determined this should not prove impossible. Its fibre has a special quality which combines strength with a remarkable softness, and there is no substitute. The other materials are simple enough. Any strong thread and a light copper wire will serve. In the binding the tightness is more important than the material. The craft needs few tools though the special *manriki* is essential.

Should you get that far, then your troubles will begin, though practice could overcome them. There is a lot of judgment needed in this craft, apart from manual skill, which helps to achieve the essential stability in the structure of the broom so that it will not wilt at the first touch of a floor. For those who need encouragement, let me quote that charming Japanese proverb: 'You become good at what you like'.

26 With the brush placed in a wooden clamp to hold the fibres in position, Ishikawa-san sews a line of stitching at a point where it will hold the brush firm when in use

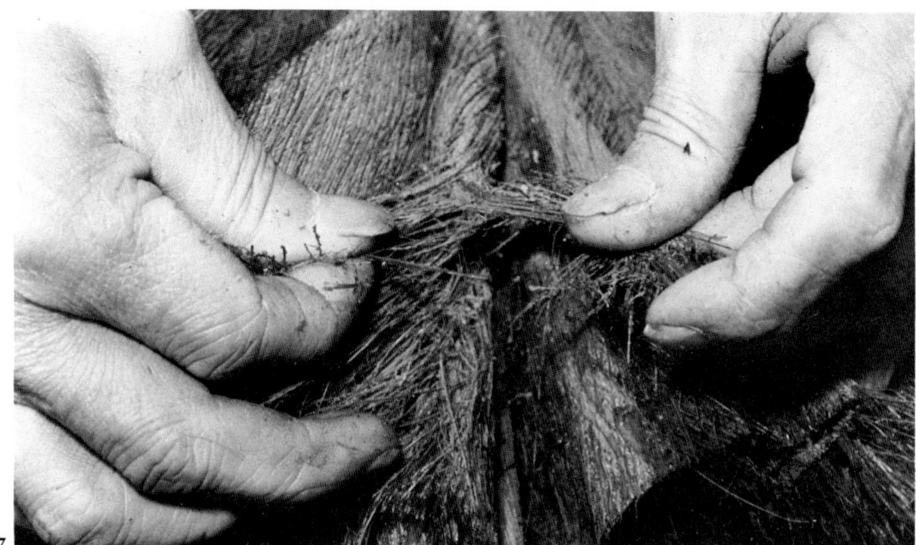

27 The fibres of the brush are separated by hand

扇子

風呂敷

櫛

Traditional
Dress

4

Folding Fans
Sensu

Two types of fan have been used by the Japanese for many centuries and have played a part in many aspects of Japanese life. The rigid fan, made in a great variety of shapes and sizes, is the older type and seems to have been introduced from China through Korea. It remains popular today both as a summer fan and in a more humble role for enlivening the charcoal fire and for cooking. The kitchen-fan's paper covering was strengthened with persimmon juice. It became a symbol of poverty and was shown held by Binbogami, the god of poverty.

The folding fan was that rare thing, a wholly Japanese invention. It appeared possibly as early as the middle of the seventh century AD, though early recorded references of 703 and 763 may refer to rigid rather than folding fans. However, at this time the fan was already an important part of formal attire for men and women and was playing an increasing part in both court and religious life. One of the earliest and most elaborate fans was the type made for the Empress and the court ladies. This was a folding fan made only of wood, its thirty-eight sticks forming the fan, with artificial flowers at the corners and decorated with twelve long silk streamers. It continued in use at the Imperial Court until the end of the Edo period in 1867.

From its early introduction, the folding fan assumed various symbolic meanings and special purposes beyond its basic ability to bring a touch of coolness in the hot summer months, from the rituals of the Imperial Court to the humbler roles of prop for the storyteller and test of the amazing skill of the Japanese juggler.

In early times the fan seems to have become a symbol of authority. The best example is the battle-fan, carried by the commander and used to give orders. Its sticks were made of cast iron and it carried on one side a red sun on a gold ground, and on the other a silver moon and stars on a black or dark blue ground. The referee at sumo-wrestling still carries a fan as a symbol of his authority, his rank denoted by the colour of the tassel.

The folding fan has also commonly been used in all forms of theatre and dance, playing an important part in Noh plays, kabuki plays and various dances. The dance fan, dating from the seventeenth century, has ten sticks and is made with thick paper usually decorated with a family crest. Large fans which open in a steep V-angle are used in Noh plays, while the kabuki fan has a stronger and more colourful decoration. Religious fans, used by Buddhist priests, are Y-shaped and many smaller fans are beautifully decorated with gold or silver sutra prayers in Japanese characters printed on a dark blue or black ground.

The fan also plays a part in many Japanese festivals, most usually the giant fans which are carried during the festival of the sun goddess at Ise, Japan's main Shinto shrine, and the firemen's festival in Kyoto. There is a fan-throwing game, and a more literary competition for the best poem written on a fan. People attending the tea ceremony must carry a fan tucked in their kimono but it is never used except possibly as a 'tray' or 'dish' for passing tea ceremony sweets or small cakes. The tea fan has only three sticks and beautiful but restrained decoration. There are also miniature fans, some for decorative use, some for children's dolls, and some with a tea bowl or vase as a wedding favour or in acknowledgment for a gift on the birth of a baby. The folding fan is an engagement present, a symbol of respect, friendship and future happiness, and today is often bought as a piece of decoration to be mounted in a room on a neat bamboo or wooden stand.

The folding fan and its basic shape have also been used in countless ways for centuries to decorate other objects. It is a common ornament for decorating textiles and paper and for sliding screens. It has long been popular as a motif on folding screens; one type is called 'screen of scattered fans'. It has decorated an enormous variety of ceramic and lacquer boxes, and many of these, from tiny pottery incense boxes to large and elaborate lacquer boxes, have been made in the shape of a folding fan.

Fans have been painted by the greatest artists of Japan. More recently, as Basil Hall Chamberlain wrote in 1904: 'Fans have been extensively used as vehicles for advertisements. . . . In these latter days, when Europeanization has corrupted everything, one has much to suffer from while fanning oneself on a hot day. Art has surely sounded its lowest depths when it comes to portraying a lager-beer bottle on one side of a fan, and to providing a railway time-table on the other.' Today, however, the fan is more seriously threatened by modern air-conditioning than by mere vulgarity.

Although the fan has lost many of its traditional uses, one is still struck as one wanders through the centre of Kyoto, the home of the fan and still the main centre of fan-making, at the large number of shops which seem to flourish on the specialist sale of fans. No doubt the majority are sold as souvenirs or as purely decorative objects, but each hot and humid summer the folding fan comes back into its own, and on the restaurant balconies that line the Kamogawa River or in the crowded kabuki theatre a multitude of fluttering fans bring pleasure to the eye and a slight coolness to the cheek. The folding fan seems likely to remain a charming feature of Japanese life for a long time to come.

For the non-Japanese the folding fan, its construction and decoration, and its long history, point to a number of interesting facts about Japan and the Japanese character. To the foreigner, indeed, it is a symbol of Japan itself, as evocative as Mount Fuji or the kimono.

The fan evokes a picture of half-concealed eyes, dark and inscrutable. In the past the fan was used by an inferior to cover the mouth when speaking to a superior person. Women still cover their mouths with their hand when they laugh. It is said that love letters were concealed in folding fans. And perhaps the fan, along with the great variety of small Japanese folding screens, helped to give a slight sense of privacy in a traditional architecture which gave none. Perhaps the folding fan once gave the Japanese the same sense of security that dark glasses give to some people today.

Part of the fascination of Japanese civilization is how from earliest times such a subtle and beautiful culture has been created through the infinite exploitation of simplicity. Japan has always been poor in native raw materials. Yet an amazingly complex art, architecture and way of life have been created from bamboo, clay, paper, rice and a few other humble indigenous materials.

The fan is a perfect example of this process. The original invention has been exploited and developed with the same kind of ingenuity that today has made Japan the leader in electronics, cameras and watches. The Japanese genius has been not so much for original creation as an extraordinary and unique gift for 'creative development'. The evolution of the fan is also wholly relevant to traditional Japanese life and the unique circumstances that have moulded Japanese society. Japan has long been short of space. Because of this, much in Japanese life has been 'miniaturized', and in those cases where the object could not be made small then, like the fan, it was made to fold. This was particularly useful with the kimono, which has no pockets, for the folding fan can be tucked neatly into the front fold or the sash, or slipped inside the deep sleeve.

The folding fan also exemplifies Japanese art and craftsmanship serving the needs of Japanese life. Humble materials – bamboo or wood combined with paper and rice-glue – are brought together with ingenuity and skill to make an object that is useful, convenient, beautiful and versatile; its versatility exploited for a score of uses, mundane and ceremonial. At the same time it has provided a vehicle for an almost infinite range of decoration and artistry, each special use defining structure and pattern.

Making a Folding Fan

Making a folding fan involves some thirty separate processes carried out by as many as six specialist craftsmen. Some of the processes are simple; several require great skill and judgment, only learned by long experience. Some craftsmen work independently; others work in a sort of syndicate organized by a leading fan-seller. The craft, its materials and its tools are extremely traditional, but since the Second World War some modern materials and tools have been introduced. The craftsmen are scattered about Kyoto, working in small, crowded workshops, either alone and assisted by their wives, or in groups of two or three. Before the War Kyoto

28 A fan-decorator's workshop

28

29

29 The gold arabesque pattern is printed on the red ground. The white shape of the paeony is still covered by a dark cut-out shape of the flower, which protected the area when the fan was painted red

craftsmen made many cheap fans for export to countries like Spain, but today most fans are made for the home market.

The two basic parts of a fan are the framework of sticks and the covering of paper; some are covered in silk, but that is a separate craft. The majority of sticks are made of bamboo, though certain kinds of Chinese wood are also used. For Kyoto fans the bamboo is grown in nearby Shiga prefecture and is cut when about three years old. Mostly *madake* bamboo is used, but sometimes *mosodake* bamboo. The cutting of the bamboo into the necessary lengths for different types of fan, the basic shaping, drying and piercing with either structural or decorative holes are all done in Shiga, after which the sticks are brought to Kyoto for the other processes. They arrive bundled and riveted into sets suitable for each type of fan, the inner sticks protected by two larger and stronger outside sticks. Correct drying for three or four days in mildly warm sun is vital, and the fining-off of the ends of the sticks to fit into the paper is a fine skill. The bamboo is either left plain or coated with black or red lacquer. Fine Chinese woods are left plain, admired for their colour and figure.

The next step is the making of the special paper, *usui* being the only kind used for folding fans. The sheets of paper are first sized, now often done by machine. Then three or five sheets of paper are laminated. The central piece of paper in this lamination is softer so that it will 'collapse' easily when the necessary holes are made to take the sticks. After lamination the paper is dried, then cut into fan-shapes of various sizes using a metal-die. These 'blanks' are bundled up for delivery to the decorator.

For centuries folding fans have been decorated with painting. Fans are still handpainted, some by famous artists, but in recent years a wide variety of techniques has been used to decorate cheaper fans. These include mass-production painting techniques – stencilling, printing, silk-screen printing – singly or in combination, the final effect heightened with gilding and silvering, either with leaf or metallic paints. The variety is almost infinite; the final effect frequently exquisite.

A typical fan-decorator's workshop is tucked away on the upper floor of a small building just south of the centre of Kyoto. It started about eighty years ago, when it was devoted to producing cheap fans for Spain. Production today is wholly for the home market. At the top of steep, narrow wooden stairs are three rooms packed from floor to ceiling with boxes of stencils, paintbrushes, fan-blanks, saucers of paint – and atmosphere.

The owner – who has worked at the craft for over fifty years – and three assistants crouch over low tables, decorating fans in a basic stencil-technique, filled out with freehand painting, gilding and silvering. Many of the fans are incredibly elaborate; one fan can take a month to stencil, print and paint, involving some five blocks for the basic pattern, outlining in black

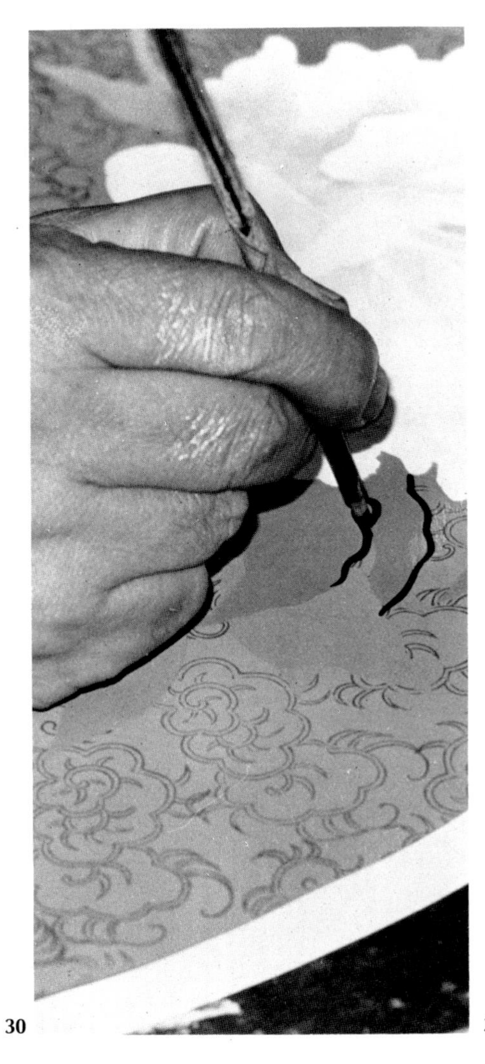

30

31

30 The detail of the flower and leaves is handpainted in black ink

31 The fan at two stages of decoration: the body of the flower painted, the gold arabesque printed and the outlines of the leaves stencilled; more detail added to the paeony and the leaves handpainted

ink, and various other painting finishes. Today these traditional effects are more and more often achieved by silk-screen printing.

In this fairly traditional workshop a typical fan is decorated as follows. The white blank is painted red, the shape of the flower decoration left uncoloured. A gold arabesque pattern is then printed over the red ground. The central flower, a paeony, is started with the *bokashi* technique, where a touch of soft pink paint is smear-rubbed over the reserved shape with a soft brush, after which the body of the flower is strengthened with various shades of pink. Next the green leaves are stencilled in and the leaf-detail is handpainted with black ink. The incredible variety of brushes used is remarkable. The paeony is finished with delicate painting in yellow of the stamen. Many of the decorative subjects are extremely traditional and the stencils of great age, carefully cleaned and dried after each painting. This one workshop had stencils for an enormous variety of patterns and designs,

32

32 The fan is folded between two moulds of folded and strengthened paper

all in frequent use as could be seen by looking at the dozens of fans drying on the string-racks which criss-crossed every inch of the ceilings.

The folding of the fans may sound a simple operation but in fact involves some seventeen processes, many extremely skilful. Tokio Kitazawa-san works assisted only by his wife in one of those deep, narrow traditional houses called in Kyoto an 'eel-house'. His workshop is neat and peaceful in comparison with the Dickensian surroundings of the fan-decorator.

Piles of decorated flat fans are delivered daily. The work is mostly done at a small, solid table. The only large tools are a few heavy, traditional presses. The first and perhaps most skilful step is to open the 'mouth' of the lower end of the edge of the fan with a small steel and bamboo knife, to allow for the later insertion of the sticks. Next the fans are wrapped in a damp cloth to make the paper more pliant for folding, after which the damp sheets are placed between two fan-shaped wooden boards. The fans are then folded between two moulds (*kata*) of folded and strengthened paper. The process is done very quickly, with the fingers pressing the folds extremely tightly and making sure that they are compact, tight and 'squared-off' perfectly. It looks absurdly simple but in fact takes years of practice to do correctly. If the folding is incorrectly done, the fan will never open or close properly. A fan-folder will have as many as forty different-sized and -shaped *kata* for a whole range of folding fans, from fans for dolls to large ceremonial and decorative fans for festivals.

33 The edges of the newly-folded fan are squared off with a wooden wedge

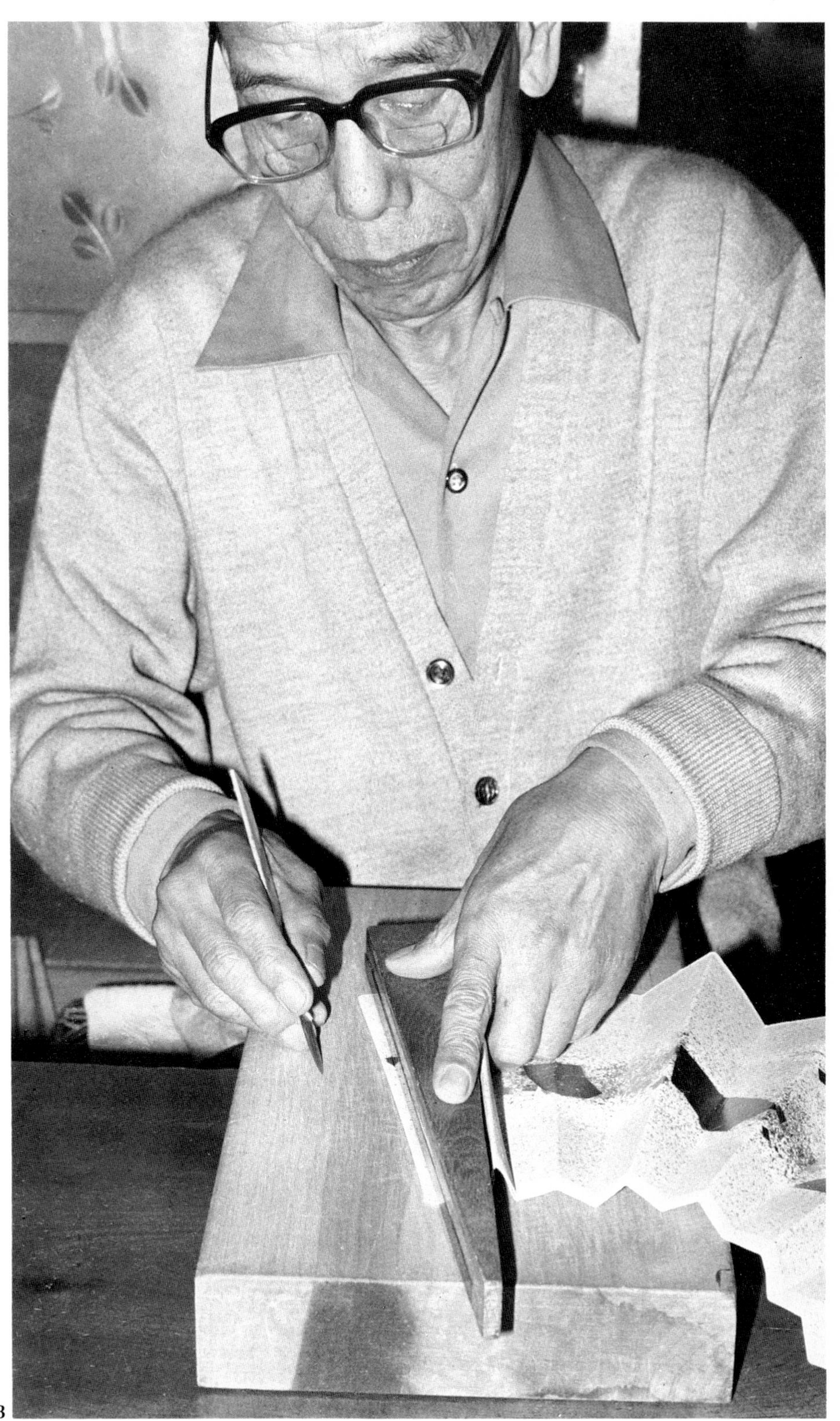

33

34 The stick holes are reopened with a bamboo spike

There follow a number of processes to ensure the correct shape of the fan and the perfect and permanent lie of the folding. The upper edge is trimmed with a knife and neatly folded over, which involves the delicate skill of cutting only halfway through the paper thickness. The exposed end-edges are glued with rice-paste and folded over to make a strong edge. In all these shaping and finishing processes heavy wooden fan-shaped wedges (*tataki*) are used, both to give the correct line and to act as simple presses, sharpening the edges of the folds with firm hammering. Finally, the folded fan is put into a simple wooden press for at least a night, the longer the better, and later hung out on a string rack for the final drying.

Next, with a flat bamboo 'spike', the stick-holes are reopened and the fans spend a second night in the press. Then, while the fan is held in a special wooden press, about 4 cm (1·6 in.) is neatly trimmed off the ends with a very sharp steel 'hatchet'. Finally the fans are made up into neat packets, ready for delivery to the workshop of the 'fan-fitter'.

Both the folded fans and the sticks are delivered to the small workshop of the fan-fitter who makes the fans ready for delivery to the fan shop. The fans arrive tied in blocks of ten. Before they are untied, the top ends are gilded – high-quality fans with gold leaf and cheaper fans with gold paint. After this the fans are separated and by blowing on the bottom edge of each fan, the stick holes are opened up, one by one.

Then the sticks for the fan are spread out and, with a wide brush, glue is spread on both sides of each stick, except for the two outside ones. The traditional rice-paste is today mixed with a modern chemical glue, the two carefully mixed on a wooden board with a wooden spatula. The glued parts of the sticks are then neatly inserted into the holes, very carefully straightened into the exactly correct position, then tapped firmly with a wooden wedge. The fan is then rechecked, and any surplus glue wiped away; it is then put into a holding-press and, with the outside sticks folded back, left to dry overnight. The following day the perfect 'squaring-up' of the fan and sticks is again checked. To prevent the body of the fan from bulging it is again beaten to make it thinner.

The final stage of attaching the two outside sticks to the two ends of the fan requires great skill. First, the inside of the two sticks and the surfaces of the ends of the fan are cleaned of all lacquer or gilding to provide a clean surface for glueing. Then, by the use of carefully controlled heat and precise bending, the two sticks must be given a slight curve so that they fit the fan exactly. The sticks can be curved after softening by heat either with a traditional press; in a 'mould' made of two strips of leather; or just with the experienced eye of the craftsman. When the fit is perfect, the ends of the two sticks are clipped to the length of the fan, and the ends are blackened. This used to be done with Chinese ink but today a felt-tip marker is used.

35 The sticks are inserted into the holes

36 The two outer sticks are gently curved with an iron

Next small paper bands, like cigar-bands, are made. The sticks are then glued to the ends of the fan, more chemical glue being used this time for quicker drying. After the sticks have been firmly pressed into position, the paper band is slipped around the completed fan to hold it in position. The fan is then left to dry for at least three hours after which it is finally checked. Before they are sold, the better-quality fans are put into paper packets, and the best in cardboard, or even wooden, boxes.

Practical Note

The processes in making a folding fan may appear reasonably simple. The real problem is that each one must be done perfectly or the fan will not open and close correctly. Exact folding and a perfect fitting of the sticks into the paper are critical. Anyone wanting to try making a folding fan would do well to start by buying a cheap Japanese fan, now easily obtainable in most countries. First examine it carefully, then take it to pieces, analysing the structure which is the same for cheap or expensive fans.

As for the materials, the correct paper will be the most difficult item to obtain, though a wide range of Japanese papers are now available. Experiment with ordinary paper until you have the correct measurements and the basic skill. The *kata* needs to be made of a thick, strong yet flexible paper. Experiment also with the lamination, remembering the importance of the soft central sheet. Do not waste efforts decorating your fan until you have mastered folding. Bamboo is best for the sticks but experiment with any wood that offers strong flexibility when cut into thin lengths. Use a strong glue as there is considerable strain when the fan is continually opened and shut in use. Be extremely careful at all stages to clean off excess glue immediately.

5

Carrying Cloths *Furoshiki*

For centuries the Japanese have carried their possessions wrapped in pieces of cloth. An illustration in a *sutra* (Buddhist scripture) of the Heian period shows people carrying their clothes in bundles on their heads in what was then called a *hirazutsumi*, literally meaning 'flat wrapping'. The word *furoshiki* first appeared in documents dating from the 1680s, and this change of name seems to have been linked with the growing popularity of the public bath-house at the time.

Furoshiki literally means 'bath-spread' (*furo* bath, *shiki* spread). In the early eighteenth century at the public bath, men bathed in a loincloth and women in a slip. After their bath they 'spread a cloth' to wrap up their wet bathing clothes. By the middle of the eighteenth century the word *hirazutsumi* had been completely replaced by *furoshiki*, although the carrying cloth was by then being used for various purposes that had nothing to do with the bath-house. The neighbourhood public bath-house still flourishes everywhere in Japan, but the *furoshiki* has been replaced by a small plastic bowl in which are carried towels and washing things. Loincloths and slips have gone as men and women now bath separately.

Merchants took to using much larger *furoshiki* to carry their stock to their customers' houses, instead of only selling from their shops. In some traditional trades this custom continues today. Kimono-sellers, haberdashers, abacus-repairers, lending libraries, medicine-sellers, all these used large *furoshiki* decorated with their trade name and badge.

During the Meiji period Western-style luggage and bags were introduced to Japan, but for most Japanese the *furoshiki* remained their standard baggage up until the end of the Second World War, and it stayed in fairly general use up until some fifteen years ago. Most Japanese homes have little storage space for large pieces of luggage and even today, certainly within Japan, the Japanese travel with remarkably little luggage. The modern Japanese hotel continues certain traditions of the older Japanese inn, providing a quick laundry service and either free or machine-dispensed razors and toothbrushes, thereby cutting the traveller's need of luggage to a minimum. Even in recent times Japanese railway stations and local airports were not geared to cope with the quantities of luggage carried by Westerners. I know from bitter experience as a tour leader that the brief stops of Japan's express 'bullet trains' do not allow time to load on a foreign group's mountain of luggage before the automatic doors start to close. However, increasing foreign travel is changing traditional habits, and today, more and more, smart sets of luggage from the right French or Italian fashion houses have become as important as the right *furoshiki* for one's kimono used to be.

In Japan the rituals of wrapping things up have depths of meaning and importance far beyond mere practical convenience. Everything must be wrapped on every occasion, and usually differently wrapped for different occasions. The elaborate etiquette of wrapping extended the use of the *furoshiki* far beyond the bath-house, the merchant's pack or as a simple form of luggage.

Even money should be wrapped before being presented. Since even large transactions in Japan, such as the purchase of a new car, are still often done in cash, vast quantities of notes change hands daily. In certain cases money is presented wrapped in beautifully decorated envelopes, with special types of decoration for wedding gifts, funeral gifts, birthday presents or whatever the occasion. This tradition goes so deep that even by your bank's computerized cash-dispenser there will be a pile of decorated envelopes in which you can wrap your own mechanically dispensed cash. In some cases money is still presented wrapped in a *furoshiki*. At Iwagaki-san's Kyoto workshop, where we made the craft study for this chapter, he showed us the smallest kind of *furoshiki*, 32 cm (12·6 in.) square and used for presenting gifts of money on formal occasions. Inside the cloth was a rectangular board, lacquered red on one side and black on the other. The red side was turned upwards for festive occasions, and the black side when making a funeral offering.

Furoshiki come in many sizes. The next size up was 47 cm (18·5 in.) square, suitable for wrapping small gifts or tuition fees. The standard, general-purpose *furoshiki* is 70 cm (27·5 in.) square, and there is one of 90 cm (35·4 in.) square which is used for carrying a folded kimono. The formal *furoshiki*, usually carried by women wearing kimono, are generally made of crêpe silk with handpainted or stencilled decoration. The very large *furoshiki*, still used for general packing, are made of cotton. Deep-blue cotton cloth decorated with 'long life' designs of crane and turtle, is used for wrapping marriage furniture and bedding. Many shops selling more traditional goods still use these extremely practical cotton *furoshiki* in delivering their goods to their customers. On occasion a shopkeeper has even lent me a *furoshiki* to take my purchases home, leaving me to return the carrying cloth when convenient.

In Japan gifts are the oil in the wheels of daily life and, to some extent, a way of avoiding becoming burdened with small obligations. The choice of exactly the right gift for the right person on the right occasion is a culture in its own right and not one likely to be mastered by any foreigner. Certainly, in traditional life gifts have provided great use for the *furoshiki*. In Japan all gifts must be wrapped, in former times in a *furoshiki*, and a gift must never be unwrapped in front of the giver, or any mention of the gift made thereafter. In opening the gift, or commenting on it, one might inadvertently give away one's genuine reaction! Since so many gifts in Japan turn out to be 'exactly what one did not want', this etiquette of silence provides admirable protection. Certain professional people, particularly doctors, are showered with expensive presents, both by grateful patients and hopeful drug companies. I know of one doctor's wife who keeps a large cupboard simply to house unwanted gifts.

Gifts are big business in Japan. Many people simply supply names and addresses with a price limit to their local department store, who have large departments to deal with seasonal gifts. There are other occasions where a single gift between two powerful company presidents may involve tremendous thought, vast expense and the employment of some specialist to seek out a suitably prestigious gift from halfway across the world. Today most gifts are beautifully packed by the shops, so a *furoshiki* is no longer required unless it is used to carry the parcel. Some shops, respecting tradition, put a pretty plastic *furoshiki* around the real packing.

Gifts must be given to many people just before the New Year and at the start of the summer, and this must often be a severe strain on the household budget. One never visits another person's house for a meal without taking a gift, in this case usually food or drink. I always used to take tins of English tea, thinking it very suitable, until a Japanese friend mentioned that tea was only suitable for funerals. I am not sure that she is correct, but for the time being I have switched to tins of English biscuits. There simply cannot be a Japanese tradition about them. Occasionally an older visitor will still bring their gift wrapped in a *furoshiki*, perhaps some homemade plum wine or special pickles, and the *furoshiki* must be returned correctly folded just as the guest is leaving. At wedding parties every guest receives a handsome present when they leave and these are still each wrapped in a cheap but decorative *furoshiki*.

The *furoshiki* is always tied diagonally, corner to corner, knotted and re-knotted as necessary. If skilfully and tightly tied, a *furoshiki* will hold a bundle of considerable size and weight with complete security, and it is a wholly practical form of luggage or packing. In Japan, all parcel-making is done diagonally and not on the square as in the West, and probably this practice comes from the way of tying the *furoshiki*. To make a perfect parcel in the Japanese way requires a near-origami technique to lose those superfluous triangles of paper that always pop out just when the folding of the paper seems complete. No doubt the square ends of the Western parcel are equally perplexing to a Japanese. Even the humblest parcel in Japan can seem a work of art. I used to return from shopping to my hotel in Tokyo eager to examine my purchases, but on many occasions when I looked again at the parcel I found it hard to open it as the wrapping seemed even more pleasing then the contents.

The general use of the *furoshiki* has undoubtedly declined in recent years and the three Kyoto workshops we visited confirmed this. Today *furoshiki*

37 Part of Iwagaki-san's dye store and workshop

are mostly sold to go with kimono, or as a popular form of souvenir. The shrinking market has made high-quality *furoshiki* expensive; one worthy of a beautiful kimono might well cost 50,000 yen or more, but that is not so much when one remembers that a fine kimono will easily cost 1 million yen. One regrets the decline of the ordinary *furoshiki*, which was a simple, flexible and extremely practical form of luggage. But as long as women wear kimono, they will want the beautiful crêpe silk *furoshiki* to go with them, an elegant fashion accessory that has come a long way from the seventeenth-century bath-house.

Time and again scarcity has been the mother of invention in Japan. It is so characteristic of Japanese to take a square of cloth and make it serve with complete efficiency for an envelope, a wallet, a handbag, a suitcase, a packing case and, on occasions, as a winter hood. And to make it so that, whatever purpose it serves, at the end of the day it can be folded away to occupy the minimum of space.

Carrying Cloths

Plate 8 Silk carrying cloths stencilled with traditional patterns. (See Chapter Five)

Wooden Combs
Plate 9 A comb from a traditional marriage set of eight combs and two pins. (See Chapter Six)

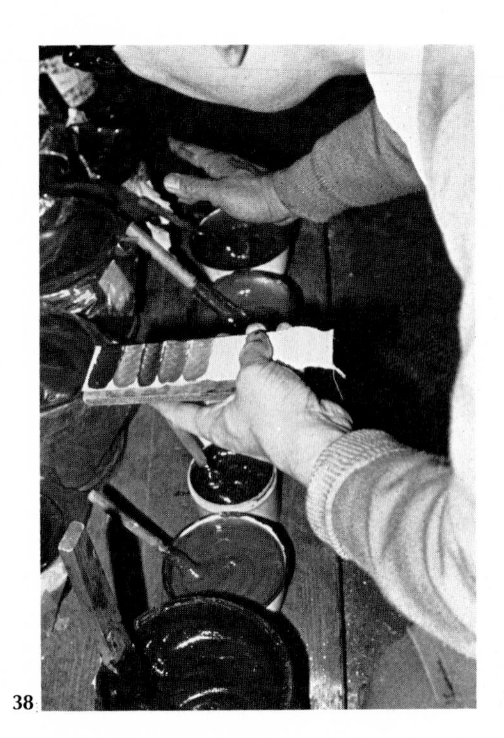

38 The colour test strips are made up

Making a Carrying Cloth

Hirotsugu Iwagaki-san is the owner of a workshop in central Kyoto where *furoshiki* are decorated with stencilled designs. His father started the firm in 1908. Iwagaki-san is now over seventy but still very much in charge of his workshops. There are various ways of decorating *furoshiki*, such as painting, stencilling and printing. The stencilled *furoshiki* made by Iwagaki-san are of the finest quality. Indeed, our introduction to him came through one of the best kimono shops in Kyoto.

The methods and processes of his craft are extremely traditional and probably little has ever changed in these workshops. They have a Dickensian air, with their low ceilings and dark corners and a rather dingy clutter everywhere. Pots and jars of every shape and size line shelves and cover the floor, the rich dyes contained in them glowing in the gloom. The stairs, as narrow and precipitous as a galleon's gangway, lead to the upper floor which is dominated by huge racks suspended from the ceiling which hold the long working-boards. Outside in the courtyard, piles of dirty stencils lie in seeming disarray. Yet, out of this apparent chaos, as always in Japanese workshops of this character, comes immaculate work. As the craftsmen move quietly about their business, never a drop of anything is spilt and somehow everyone knows exactly where everything is.

The long lengths of white crêpe silk from which the *furoshiki* are made are bought in from another company. Iwagaki-san's workshop only decorates them. The special dyes are mixed on the premises under the personal supervision of Iwagaki-san. Great care is taken with colour selection and matching, particularly when using traditional patterns. Today, almost without exception, chemical dyes are used which were first imported from Germany in about 1900. The dyes are mixed with a glue made from rice flour, rice bran and salt. This glue is now also made elsewhere. Sometimes a small cake of wheat glutin is added to the dye.

To obtain exactly the right colour, Iwagaki-san first mixes small quantities of the dye and makes up 'colour test strips' in a corner of his workshop. These strips are then put into a special steaming-pot, to subject the dyes to the same treatment that the whole *furoshiki* will receive during the full dyeing process. After a certain time the strips are removed, dried and the colours checked. To some extent the colours are seasonal: dark for winter, pale for spring. But many of the designs are suitable for all seasons. Popular is the design of pine, bamboo and plum, symbolizing good luck, and a design composed of various lucky emblems is considered suitable for marriage.

The lengths of crêpe silk are now pinned to long boards made of pine wood. Each board is about 6 metres long and 1 metre wide, taking enough silk to make eight *furoshiki*. To make maximum use of the limited space the

39

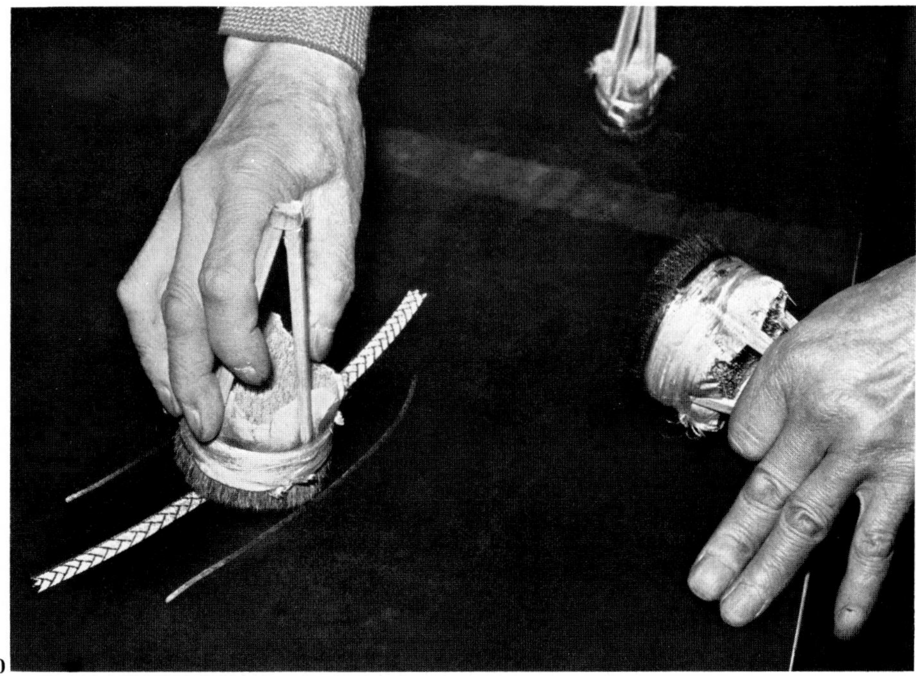

40

39, 40 The two methods of applying dye to the silk through the stencil: *left*, with a scraper; *right*, with a brush

silk is pinned to both sides of the board. Iwagaki-san only makes these high-quality silk *furoshiki*. Cheaper ones are made of cotton, nylon and a thin summer cloth called *ro*, usually with printed decoration. In fact, with the shrinking market, the main demand is now for silk *furoshiki* as it is becoming uneconomic to make cheaper kinds.

The stencils are of a traditional kind used for centuries in Japan. They are made of a special, extremely strong Japanese paper called *kata-gami*. Three sheets are layered together by brushing them with the juice of unripe persimmon fruit. They are dried in the sun, and then smoked for several days. The process is repeated and the paper is then stored for two or three years. The paper stencils used by Iwagaki-san are further strengthened with black lacquer on the back, and with silk gauze supporting the cut-out areas.

An elaborate design, using several colours, can require a set of between twenty to thirty stencils. A set of fifteen stencils might cost about 80,000 yen. They are cut by specialist craftsmen and bought in by Iwagaki-san. Many of the designs he uses are wholly traditional, and even his new designs are in a traditional style. Since his *furoshiki* will mostly be used by women wearing kimono, their designs must accord with the highly traditional kimono designs.

The dyes are applied to the silk through the stencils either with a scraper, or with a small stubby brush, and rubbed into the silk. Iwagaki-san's craftsmen are mostly middle-aged but they place the stencils and apply the dyes with remarkable precision and speed, setting down each stencil in

Wooden Combs
Plate 10 The two delicate hairpins from a traditional set of combs
Plate 11 A boxwood comb. (See Chapter Six)

Paper Umbrellas
Plate 12 Exploiting the structure of the paper umbrella for decorative effect. (See Chapter Seven)

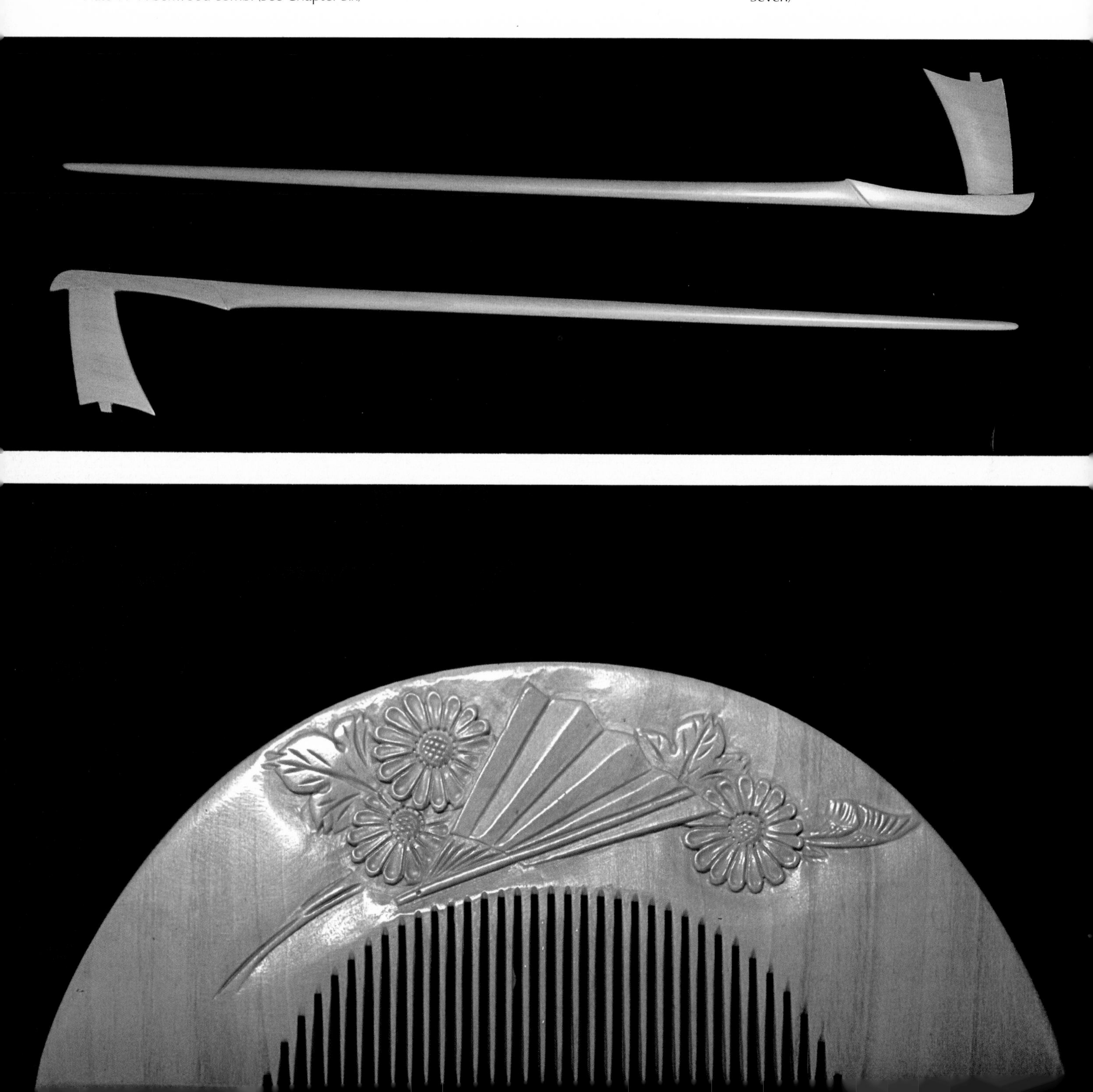

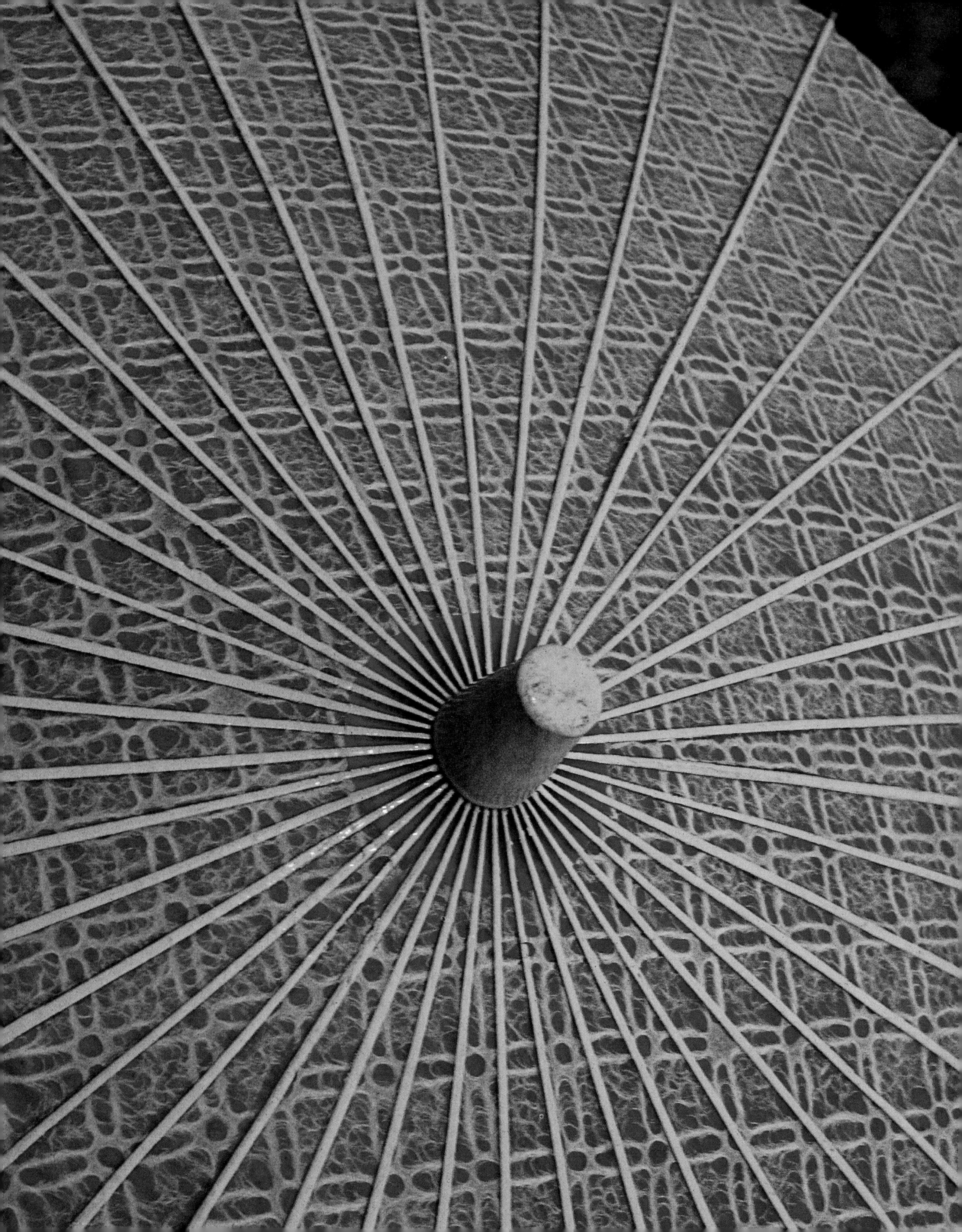

41 The wooden tank used for washing the stencils

42 The boards racked overhead for drying

exactly the correct position without the slightest hesitation even though some of the patterns are extremely complicated. After one side is finished, the board is turned over and the silk on the other side stencilled. Then the long boards are stacked vertically in the ceiling-racks above the stencilling benches and left to dry. A special wooden tank is used to wash the stencils which must always be kept slightly moist, sometimes a problem in the summer.

When the lengths of silk are dry, they are removed from the boards and cut into individual *furoshiki*. These are now mounted on small wooden racks for the steaming which will fix the dyes. The racks are placed inside a steam oven made of cedar wood, previously heated by coal, but today by oil. The steam comes up through the floor of the oven, which is covered with a straw mat to ensure even distribution of the steam. The temperature reaches about 100°C, in which the *furoshiki* are steamed for twenty-five minutes. After being taken out of the oven, they are washed and dried and prepared for packing. The steam oven, an impressive-looking piece of traditional equipment, only lasts for five years.

43 Having been cut, the individual *furoshiki* are hung on small racks for steaming

Practical Note

The first time I ever saw a *furoshiki* was long before I had visited Japan. I was spending an evening with Bernard Leach and he showed us how he could carry some twelve pieces of his pottery in one Japanese carrying-cloth. From that moment I have never ceased to admire the usefulness of the *furoshiki*, and would recommend it to everyone, and particularly to craftsmen as a convenient and pleasing way of carrying tools, craft objects or just odds and ends. For obvious reasons, an exact imitation of Iwagaki-san's processes is difficult but there are many simple and attractive ways of decorating a *furoshiki*, and many books available with suitable Japanese designs. Both the decoration and the finished object might be particularly suitable for children – who would want a mere lunchbox if they could carry their lunch to school in a *furoshiki*?

Paper Umbrellas

Plate 13 Oiled paper umbrellas set out to dry in the sun

Plate 14 The inner mechanism of a paper umbrella interwoven with bright silk thread. (See Chapter Seven)

6

Wooden Combs
Kushi

The earliest combs found in Japan appear to have been hair ornaments. Combs for combing the hair may only have been introduced through Chinese example during the Nara period. From then on combs were used for both purposes in Japan, though fashions varied from period to period. From the seventeenth century combs of both sorts were produced in great variety and traditional combs remained popular up to the Second World War. Since then, the general adoption of Western dress and the introduction of mass-produced combs and electric gadgets for hair-care has sharply reduced the market for traditional combs.

There remains a limited market for the traditional type of boxwood comb described later in this chapter and a large number of special wooden combs are made for weavers. There are also still a few specialized markets: the combs needed by hairdressers creating traditional hairstyles for geisha and the wigs worn at weddings and in the kabuki theatre; and the sets of combs made for certain Shinto shrines. Kimono are still widely worn on such special occasions as weddings or festivals but ornamental combs are no longer fashionable.

Fragmentary remains of what was almost certainly a kind of ornamental comb have been found, thought to date from 1000 BC or earlier. These may have been used by either men or women for holding their long hair in place and, like all pre-Nara combs, they are small and narrow with long teeth. There may also have been practical combs at this early period but the material evidence is fragmentary until the shorter and wider type of comb was introduced from China during the Nara period. From that time there were combs for combing the hair; combs for securing the woman's chignon and the man's topknot (the hair first dampened with water); combs with closer teeth for cleaning the hair; and in later times ornamental combs and matching pins for women's hair.

From the late seventeenth century elaborate hairstyles for women developed which included richly decorated combs and pins – styles seen in the Japanese prints of the eighteenth and early nineteenth centuries. Still today, the geisha's hairstyle is so elaborate and so easily disarranged that one of the first things a girl must learn in training to be a geisha is to sleep with a wooden neck-pillow which will not spoil her hair.

During the Edo period many different materials were used to make combs, particularly ornamental ones. Lacquered combs were particularly popular, with red lacquer becoming the height of fashion in the second half of the eighteenth century. They were enriched with painted decoration and inlaid with mother-of-pearl. Tortoiseshell became popular in the late seventeenth century, but these combs were so expensive they soon lost favour. Imitations were made using buffalo horn. Other combs were made of boxwood, *isu* wood, sandalwood, bamboo, ivory, deer horn, whale fin, silver, copper and even glass. Many of the Edo types continued to be used in the later nineteenth century, though Meiji styles, under Western influence, were less elaborate.

This chapter was based on several visits to the famous Kyoto comb shop, Jyūsan-ya, founded by a samurai family in 1869, and to the workshops of the present owner and 5th Master, Michikazu Takeuchi-san. He was extremely generous with both his time and knowledge. Among the many interesting combs in his stock and collection were three different traditional sets, partly practical, partly ornamental.

The first set was one of a sort made only for the Empresses of Japan. There were six combs and four hairpins. They were made of a dark wood and were only worn on special occasions, such as an official visit to a Shinto shrine. Second was a traditional pre-Second World War marriage set which included eight combs and two delicate hairpins. One comb had fine, close-set bamboo teeth, to clean the oil from a woman's hair. Third and most fascinating was the set of thirteen practical combs, of varied shape and size, for the traditional hairdresser. Such a set would still be necessary for dressing a geisha's hair or a marriage wig. The need for so many combs is partly explained by a list in the 'Japanese Encyclopedia' of similar combs whose uses include such niceties as combing sidelocks, sharpening sidelocks, scratching the crown of the head, and even one for supporting the sidelocks during the bath. It is small wonder that in the wake of this complex tradition, a modern haircut and shampoo, even for a man, usually takes well over an hour!

The greatest pride of Jyūsan-ya is a set of ninety-one combs in special boxes which they must make every twenty years for the Grand Shrine at Ise. Each twenty years a new shrine is built, in an identical centuries-old style. At the same time all the regalia, dedicated to the god, must be replaced in an act of renewal and purification. This includes combs, which have had a sacred significance from early times. The sets of combs that Jyūsan-ya send to Ise, and to some other Shinto shrines, must be made entirely by hand and by wholly traditional methods with no variation in design.

Both legend and history show that combs play a special part in Japanese beliefs and superstitions. It is said that in prehistoric times there was a belief that the soul of the wearer lived within the teeth of the comb that fixed the hair, and there are many later myths and practices that enforce this idea of a person's identity somehow being in their comb. Traditionally, a woman inserted a comb in her hair at marriage and threw it away if she wanted a divorce. Some Japanese people dislike being given a comb and will not pick up a lost comb, nervous that it might be 'possessed' in some way. In Okinawa, where there are different traditions from the main islands, when a woman got married, she went with her nurse to the bridegroom's house

Seal-Engraving
Plate 17 The face of a 'male' seal cut by Clifton Karhu. (See Chapter Nine)

Left
Writing and Painting Brushes
Plate 15 A selection of writing brushes.
Plate 16 Three writing brushes mounted in bamboo handles. (See Chapter Eight)

where the nurse put a comb in the bride's hair to show that the bride now belonged to the god of the bridegroom's house.

Other legends indicate that for a long time the comb has been a charm against evil powers, perhaps offering the protection of Shinto gods. A typical legend tells of a peasant woman who was swallowed by a snake but managed to kill it by sticking her comb in its throat. Another association with Shinto was the Heian practice of giving a comb to Imperial Princesses about to devote themselves to the god at Ise; in this case a symbol of their detachment from the world. Finally, that feeling of identity with one's comb is seen in the annual Comb Festival at Kyoto's Yasui Shrine. Each September women present their old combs to the shrine, a mixture of respect and perhaps a reluctance to throw away a possession which might contain something of oneself; they probably feel it is safer to place it in a Shinto shrine.

For all their conformity and uniformity, the Japanese are as full of contradictions as most people. One of these lies in modern attitudes to dress and fashion, in which hair-styling for both men and women plays an important part. From the earliest age Japanese are rigorously trained to be self-effacing and deprecatingly modest. In Japanese conversation the pronoun 'I' is avoided as much as possible and personal opinions and preferences only expressed obliquely. In personal behaviour, individuality and any form of 'showing off' is strongly disapproved of. In total contradiction to this the fashions and hairstyles that one sees every day on the streets of larger cities could not by any standards be considered self-effacing. In Japan, both men and women are intensely fashion-conscious and, more surprisingly, many young Japanese girls revel in bizarre fashions which are clearly at odds with their innate modesty and lack of real sophistication.

As for the modern hairdresser, he may not have a set of thirteen combs, but these have been replaced with other equipment of equal elaboration and techniques of equal skill. And the paraphernalia of these modern shrines is equally available to men or women. I have several times sat having a haircut while the young man in the next chair was having an intricate perm created with electrical equipment no doubt packed with Japanese technology. The cost of such fashion-styling must be enormous as even a straightforward haircut is expensive.

There are many other contradictions of this kind in Japanese society, and perhaps the solution lies in the word 'traditional'. In any area of life that still basically belongs to Japanese tradition such as personal behaviour, traditional rules, such as modesty, still apply. But where modern elements have intruded, as in fashion, creating new areas that do not fit the traditional patterns, licence is both allowed and taken.

Making a Wooden Comb

Michikazu Takeuchi-san's home and workshops are in the town of Otsu, a few miles east of Kyoto. We were welcomed by several members of his family and admired his old father's fine display of Japanese chrysanthemums. Although the family can still produce the highest-quality handmade wooden combs, today many of them are produced by the modern machinery which fills their workshops and are only finished by hand. Even the combs made largely by machine are expensive and, with a contracting market, this is one of the traditional crafts with a less certain future.

The craft described here is the making of a simple type of boxwood comb by traditional handmade methods. More elaborate combs and hair ornaments are made in basically the same way.

The preparation of the boxwood is of the utmost importance. The box trees are grown at Kagoshima in the southern island of Kyushu, although some cheaper combs are made of boxwood from Thailand. The Japanese trees must grow for at least thirty years before they reach the necessary diameter of about 22 cm (8·7 in.). Takeuchi-san goes down to Kagoshima once a year to select four or five trees, a year's supply. They are dug out by the roots which are left on until it is ready for sawing to protect the lower half of the trunk, which provides the wood for the combs. The upper trunk is used for making the beads of the Japanese abacus and the counters in *shogi*, Japanese chess.

44 Two bundles of boxwood wedges, bound together with steel bands for drying and storage

44

The lower trunk is cut into short circular sections. Each of these is sawn up into numerous small wedges which will be shaped into the combs. Sawing used to be done by hand but now is done by machine. To get the grain of the wood right for the best combs, the wedges should be cut like slices of cake, from the outer circumference of the log to its centre, but this is difficult and takes longer. Usually the log is cut right across with a sufficiently angled cut to produce wedge-shaped slices. The wedges are then dried in the sun for ten days.

This drying tends to warp the wedges. To straighten them, about fifty are bound together in a bundle, formerly with a bamboo tie but today with a band of steel. Several bundles are placed in a large oven and smoked in their own sawdust, the drying process varying from one day to two weeks. It is vital to get all the processes of drying exactly right so that the wood is completely stable. When the bundles are removed from the oven they are tightened again by driving in an oak wedge and then the wedges are stored for at least five years.

When fully seasoned, the wedges are sorted and several will be discarded. The craftsman then takes a wedge of boxwood, about 16 cm (6·3

45 The wedge is smoothed with a wooden plane

in.) long, 4 cm (1·6 in.) high and 8 cm (3·1 in.) wide at the base, and smoothes the surfaces with a wooden plane. Next he cuts the teeth of the comb with a simple bow-saw. The comb must be held completely steady, and the special vice is bedded in a slab of stone. The vice holds the comb-wedge angled away from the craftsman, and the saw blade is thick enough to cut the correct space between each tooth. The space between each tooth is made by three separate saw cuts. First, a 45-degree cut is made on one side of the wedge, and a similar cut is then made from the other side. Finally, a third cut is sawn straight downwards to meet the apex of the two angled cuts. All of this is highly skilled and done by eye. The slightest slip of the hand or vibration of the comb would split or tear the fine teeth.

When all the teeth have been sawn, they must be filed. First, a thin iron file is used and the finish is given by a wooden file on which are pasted small sheets of a dried grass called *tokusa*, soaked in water before use. Formerly sharkskin was used. Once the teeth are finished, the rectangular wedge is given a slightly curving top by sawing, filing and sandpapering.

Finally, the comb must be polished to bring out the rich sheen of the boxwood that makes these combs so beautiful. The whole comb is first rubbed over with rolls of *tokusa*, and then with leaves of the *muku* tree, again soaked before use. Finally, a small brush made of palm-hemp (see Chapter Three) is used to bring up the final polish and get between the teeth. When in use, the combs should be slightly oiled to keep both their colour and condition. Small combs of this kind, which are practical and pleasant to use, are normally sold in a fabric case of traditional design. Most are probably sold today as souvenirs to the Japanese tourists visiting Kyoto.

46

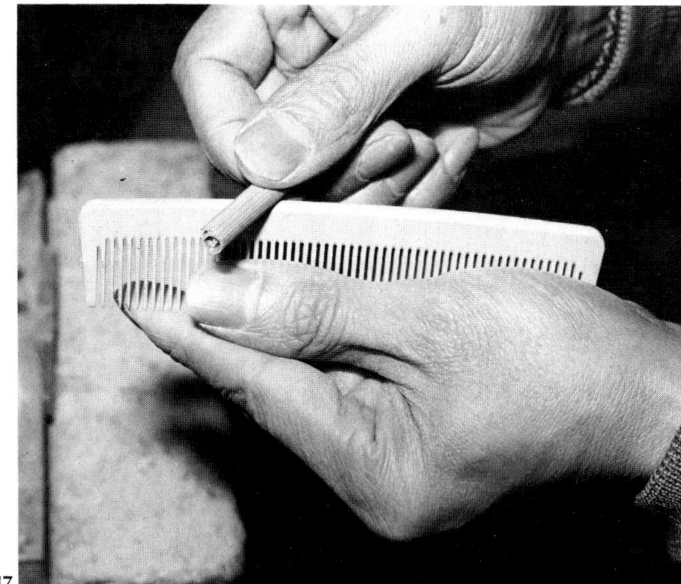

47

46 The long iron file which is used for cleaning the teeth of the comb after sawing

47 The shaped comb is polished with a roll of *tokusa* grass

Practical Note

Takeuchi-san stressed again and again that the correct preparation of the boxwood was as important as the craftsmanship in making one of these combs. The processes are basically simple, but require experience and accuracy. Anyone considering making a comb must obtain some extremely hard and stable wood. Box can, with difficulty, be obtained in the West but is now extremely expensive.

7

Paper Umbrellas
Karakasa

The paper umbrella, so much part of the European image of Japan, was not a Japanese invention. Even the origin of the Japanese word, *karakasa,* is uncertain. The word is used to distinguish it from *kasa* which once referred to straw hats which gave protection from the rain along with capes made of layers of straw. Today *karakasa* is reserved for paper umbrellas, though there are several kinds of these. The Western umbrella is *kōmongasa,* while *kasa* refers to any kind of umbrella.

There are three usual explanations of the origin of the word *karakasa,* each suggesting a different way in which the folding, paper umbrella came to Japan. *Kara* can mean a stick and it is suggested that primitive umbrellas were first made by putting straw hats on the ends of sticks. There seem to have been 'umbrellas' of this kind as early as the Nara period. *Kara* can also mean China or Korea, and it is possible that the umbrella came originally from China, or via Korea. There is said to be a record of a Korean king giving the Emperor an umbrella in AD 552. This would have been a *kinugasa,* a ceremonial umbrella for the nobility, different colours denoting different status. Umbrellas of this kind with long handles were used by the nobility and priests in the Kamakura and Muromachi periods. Finally, *kara* can mean mechanism, and it is said that a merchant from Sakai, in Osaka, in 1594, brought back this kind of umbrella from the Phillipines and presented one to Toyotomi Hideyoshi. Such uncertain origins are typical of traditional everyday Japanese objects, mainly because records of such mundane things were seldom kept.

Without doubt, a number of different forms of paper umbrella became popular with all classes during the Edo period, though in 1718 the Tokugawa government forbade the common people from using umbrellas with long handles, perhaps because of their aristocratic associations. As a result, umbrellas with short handles became popular, some for protection against the rain, and others, as parasols, against the sun.

An elegant umbrella called *janomegasa* was particularly popular with priests and doctors at the end of the seventeenth century. In the early eighteenth century a strong and cheap umbrella, with thick spokes and covered in white paper, began to be sold in Osaka and, being stronger and cheaper than former umbrellas, it quickly became popular all over Japan. But by about 1735 fashion preferred a more elegant umbrella with thinner spokes. By the late eighteenth century the spokes were even thinner and when the rain stopped people tucked these light umbrellas into the backs of their sashes. Stronger umbrellas became popular again in the early nineteenth century but they were of higher quality than those made previously in Osaka. As umbrellas became more popular, umbrella pedlars appeared who bought old umbrellas, cleaned and repapered them, and then resold them. In Edo (Tokyo) pedlars paid money for old umbrellas, but the Osaka pedlars exchanged them for such things as pots and pans.

Parasols or sunshades also became popular in the late seventeenth century, particularly with women and children. These were brightly decorated with flowers and birds. Doctors and Confucian scholars preferred a plain blue parasol. In 1749 the use of parasols, particularly by men, was prohibited again, but by the end of the Edo period, in the mid-nineteenth century, they were once more fashionable with both sexes.

Since the eighteenth century Gifu, a large town north of Nagoya, has been the main centre of paper umbrella-making and this study was made there. Gifu was originally a castle-town situated on the Nakasendo Highway and has remained an important centre of communications. Ieyasu, the first Shogun, recognizing its importance, gave the surrounding land to his eldest daughter's husband. Umbrella-making developed there about 1760 and later, when the local lord lacked money, he encouraged even poor samurai to make umbrellas. Samurai and local tradesmen specialized in the various processes and improved the techniques. After the Meiji period the industry developed enormously and by 1900 Gifu was producing one million paper umbrellas each month. But since the Second World War, with changing ways of life, and with many cheap paper umbrellas imported from Taiwan, Gifu only makes some 150,000 paper umbrellas each year.

There are several types of paper umbrella, each one for a different purpose, varying in diameter or length of spokes and length of handle. The *bangasa* is a strongly-made practical umbrella covered with white paper, with spokes 64 and 66 cm (25·1 and 26 in.) long. The *kogasa* is a shorter form of the *bangasa*. The large umbrella used for temple ceremonies and the outdoor tea ceremony is called *ogasa*. The *higasa* is a small parasol; and the *maigasa*, which may be covered with paper or silk, is used in Japanese dancing. This list is by no means exhaustive.

Despite the decline of the paper umbrella, it still has a role in Japanese life. The geisha and maiko (geisha in training) still use them, and at traditional restaurants they are often offered to guests for walking in the garden. Many parents buy a paper umbrella to go with their daughter's set of wedding kimonos, though it is most unlikely that it will ever actually be used. Monks and priests also continue to use simple paper umbrellas. A considerable number are also sold to tourists each year. It is surprising how many shops in the centre of Kyoto still sell paper umbrellas.

Although it is the Western-style umbrella which has driven out the traditional paper umbrella, certain traditional attitudes still influence both the design and use of the modern umbrella and Japan remains a land of umbrellas. From the spring to the beginning of winter, the Japanese climate is marked by sudden showers of rain. These are common throughout the hot summer when any kind of raincoat would be most uncomfortable. So the umbrella is the most effective and convenient protection, almost essential to survival in Japan. Since the Second World War Japanese ingenuity has gone to work on the umbrella, producing perfectly practical umbrellas that will fit into a small handbag yet which, with a touch of a button, spring into immediate action.

So much are umbrellas part of life, that hotels loan them to guests, many establishments offer locking racks for them, and everywhere provides a place to leave a wet umbrella, or at least a thin plastic bag in which the dripping object may be encased. Perhaps influenced by the more decorative *karakasa*, the Japanese seem less conservative about the colours of their umbrellas. Women still rejoice in bright designs while Japanese men often use umbrellas whose brightness would embarrass men in the West. For the conservative Japanese male a green or blue umbrella is commoner than black. Parasols are still commonplace, for most Japanese women do not wish their face or any part of their body to be touched by the sun's rays.

Rain, preferably light rain, is beautiful to the Japanese, and has certain romantic associations. It would not be surprising to hear a Japanese say: 'We went to the Moss Garden today and luckily it rained for a short while'. Rain not only adds various enchantments to the view, but in a sense offers a new view, for the garden with rain is different from the garden without rain. At that famous Moss Garden in Kyoto, there is an avenue of maples which offers exquisite autumn colouring, but the full delicacy can only be appreciated after a sudden shower has broken the autumn sunshine, leaving each red, gold or orange leaf sparkling with raindrops.

For young Japanese, rain and umbrellas have two special romantic associations. In the West lovers put their initials beside a heart pierced with Cupid's arrow. In Japan young lovers' initials shelter beneath an open umbrella. This seems linked with the romantic concept of *amayadori*, a meeting in the rain where two young strangers share an umbrella. A popular song of this name was a great hit a few years ago. At the first meeting under the umbrella the boy notes with love and pity that the girl has a bad tooth, and on her first visit to his house his protective feelings are intensified by the large hole in her sock. Such are the consequences of sharing a Japanese umbrella!

To the Japanese rain has a special significance. For centuries the rice crop depended on it. And in Shinto water is a sacred element. Rain is a part of that deep feeling for the changing seasons which still regulates Japanese life and affects so many daily attitudes. Even the hardened city dweller retains the countryman's sense of and almost reverence for the seasons. Within the spring blossom and the autumn leaf are interlocked pleasure and sadness, for the very fleetingness of each season, each one blessed with its special beauties and pleasures, continually underlines that Japanese sense of the transitoriness of life itself.

At a less profound level, but reflecting those basic attitudes, the changing seasons control, or at least influence, large areas of everyday life in Japan, both within the home and outside. The seasons have fixed dates which frequently bear no relation to the prevailing weather. Autumn starts early in September on which date, regardless of sun and temperature, all public swimming pools close. Within these defined seasons clothes change, bedding changes, cushion covers are changed, porcelain gives way to pottery, stationery is decorated with appropriate motifs, and food follows the seasons with exact obedience. Perhaps attitudes are becoming slightly less rigid, particularly among the young, but the sense of season and the variety it provides is still one of the pleasures of living in Japan.

Making a Paper Umbrella

48 A bundle of handles, each fitted with its top knob, awaiting assembly

The Japanese paper umbrella may appear as fragile as a butterfly, but in fact it is as strong as the bamboo from which it is made. And it gives effective protection against heavy rain. This craft involves about twenty separate processes, many carried out in different workshops. Since some of these require such particular skill and materials, this is one of the few crafts in this book beyond the ability of most Western craftsmen.

It was not possible to see every process demonstrated by the particular specialist craftsman. The large workshop we visited in Gifu now imports many ready-made umbrella frames from Taiwan, and much of their work was assembly and finishing. This did enable us to examine all the component parts and to see a number of the processes. Most important, in Gifu we were able to visit one of the best-known paperers. His craft skill, together with the beauty of the Japanese umbrella, justifies its inclusion in the book.

The construction of these umbrellas is simple yet intricate. They are made from four materials: bamboo, oiled paper, cotton and silk thread, and a coat of lacquer. The construction is basically the same as for a modern umbrella and if you keep one open in front of you, it may help you follow this description.

The bamboo used for umbrellas is *madake*, the same as for the Japanese flute (see Chapter Twelve). *Madake* is strong and does not warp or split. For umbrella-making it is cut from October to December when the wood has hardened and is most resistant to attack by insects. At the time it is cut the lengths are marked with a knife to ensure that later the structure of the umbrella frame follows the natural growth and strength of the bamboo. The bamboo is thoroughly dried and stored until needed.

49 A finished umbrella, showing how the forty-eight spokes are fitted between the wooden teeth of the top knob, and how the levers have been split to be fitted to the spokes

To simplify the description of the construction of the frame I have used Western terms for the various parts; in this craft the Japanese terms are confusing. The umbrella frame consists of five components. (Measurements are not given since, as already explained, they vary with each type of umbrella or parasol.) First there is the bamboo or wooden handle. Fixed to the top of the handle is a turned knob of wood, its bottom side cut like a cog-wheel with 49 teeth and 48 spaces between them. Another turned cylinder of wood, with a hole through its centre, slides up and down the handle. The top of this cylinder is also cut like a cog-wheel, again with 49 teeth and 48 spaces.

Now, with great exactitude, the bamboo lengths are cut to make 48 straight spokes to which eventually the paper covering will be glued. The outer ends of the spokes are bored with tiny holes and a cotton thread, the length of the circumference of the open umbrella, is threaded through them. The top ends of the 48 spokes are then placed into the 48 spaces

50 The whole bamboo frame assembled on the handle

between the teeth of the knob on top of the handle and secured by strong thread which is passed through tiny holes previously bored in both the tops of the spokes and the teeth. Thus the spokes are hinged to the bottom of the knob on top of the umbrella handle.

Forty-eight straight levers are also cut from the bamboo, about half the length of the spokes but otherwise the same size. The bottom ends of the levers are now inserted between the teeth on the sliding cylinder and hinged to it with thread in the same way. The other ends of these levers have been carefully split to a length of 4 cm (1·6 in.). These split ends are then each fitted to the spokes, about one-third of the way down the spoke, and again hinged by a continuous length of thread passing through tiny holes previously bored at this point in both the spokes and split levers.

Now, by moving the sliding cylinder up and down the handle, the frame will open and close, although at this stage, without paper or additional threading, it is a precarious operation. Within the handle, like a modern

51

51 Masuda-san, the paperer, sets each spoke and each lever in exactly the correct position around the circumference of the umbrella

umbrella, a triangular clip holds the umbrella open. This is made of bamboo, and often paper umbrellas have an upper and a lower clip which will hold the umbrella either partly or fully open.

The assembled frames are now sent in bundles to the paperer's workshop. It was Toshikazu Masuda-san who so generously demonstrated his craft. It was a memorable afternoon. Of all the craft-skills I have seen in Japan, in many ways this was the most remarkable. Were that not enough, Masuda-san's semi-dark, cramped and unbelievably cluttered workshop had a fascinating Dickensian air. To take many of the photographs it was necessary to stand behind Masuda-san, but the floor was ankle-deep in 'things'; in that light it could have been precious tools and materials or was it merely a century of unswept rubbish? The photographer stood balanced for two hours on a pile of telephone directories, the only stable surface available. The slightly bizarre character of the workshop was only rivalled by

52

52 The first strip of paper has been pasted over the bottom thread, holding the spokes in position

the character of Masuda-san himself, his steady hand and power of concentration untouched by age which, from his appearance, must have been considerable. The room and the man were one, linked by a lifetime of dedication and skill, his name a hallmark of excellence throughout his trade. I walked into one of the best umbrella shops in Kyoto the other day and happened to mention his name. Immediately the girl turned and pointed to a pile of umbrellas, the most expensive. 'Those are his,' she said.

Masuda-san settled to work. Holding an umbrella frame in his hand, he gently opened it and spread the spokes and levers in groups around the circumference threads. He fixed the handle into a sloping rack on his worktable with the top of the umbrella sloped towards him. Working entirely by eye, carefully he spread out both the spokes and the levers to their correct positions with the umbrella fully opened. The spokes were now in position to be glued and to receive the paper, yet at this stage Masuda-san must glue flimsy paper in exactly the right position on to a surface with little more substance or stability than thin air! It is one of those things that, although I have seen done, I shall never quite believe.

He started by glueing, in sections, a narrow strip of paper around the outer circumference of the frame, placing the strip centrally over the thread running through the ends of the spokes. Next, again in sections, he glued another narrow strip around the encircling thread where the levers were hinged to the spokes. Now, all the time applying his rice paste to the frame, he laid on the paper in segments, covering the main part of the frame, from where the spokes and levers joined, down to the outer circumference, leaving 1 cm (0·4 in.) of each spoke tip uncovered.

The best paper is *kozo*, a mulberry paper which should be made in the winter in cold river water. The paper is thin but extremely strong and, when tightened by oiling, holds the frame together and gives the whole umbrella

53 A strip of paper is pasted in sections around the upper thread where the spokes and levers meet

54 The main surface of the umbrella is pasted in sections. Note that the upper part of each section of paper allows for an overlap

55 The papering of the inner circle, showing the tool that is used throughout the glueing process to press each segment of paper firmly to the spokes

53

considerable strength. Papers of various colours are used for different types of umbrella. Here Masuda-san was making a fashionable umbrella with a beautiful rich purple paper.

Next the inner circle was papered. In glueing, a tool is used to press each segment of paper to the spoke, ensuring a firm fixing and also that the paper will fold along the spokes when the umbrella is lowered. It is essential to make a waterproof joint where the paper meets the knob on top of the handle. First, before papering this section, Masuda-san bound the knob with a strip of paper, and then the ends of the top segments were secured and bound again with further strips to the knob. Finally, a cap of oiled paper, or a piece of plastic, is tied to the knob, to prevent rain penetration.

Then Masuda-san closed the umbrella and checked that the folds were tight and that it closed perfectly, the papering in no way interfering with the mechanical action of the frame. The tightness of the folding is the sign of a high-quality Japanese paper umbrella as opposed to the bulging one finds in the imported Taiwanese umbrellas.

The final stages are carried out elsewhere, some at the central workshop we visited. Depending on the type and quality of the umbrella, silk threads are interwoven between the spokes and the levers for added strength and decoration. The outside of the umbrella can be decorated in a variety of ways, though the decoration of high-quality umbrellas is usually restrained. Some umbrellas, and parasols, are covered with a decorative paper, contrasting colours may be combined in papering the frame, or paper motifs in a different colour applied afterwards. Patterns, flowers, birds and so on can be painted on to the paper covering but these highly decorated umbrellas are usually intended for the tourist market. In Japan the umbrella will almost always be used when wearing kimono and the umbrella should only act as a foil, not a rival or distraction.

54

55

In some expensive umbrellas, for an additional decorative effect, the outer ends of the spokes are split and glued to the paper divided, adding an attractive feature to this decorative skeleton. It should be remembered that when the paper umbrella is in use the light passing through it makes the silhouette of the frame a major part of the umbrella's decorative character. It is this very transparency that makes it so much more beautiful than the solid modern umbrella.

Finally, the paper is oiled on the outside, today using tung oil. Then rows of umbrellas, their handles secured in holes in the ground, are stood in the sun to dry, one of the prettiest sights in Gifu. After this, with each umbrella tightly closed, black or red lacquer is painted on with a brush so that the umbrella gives the appearance, when closed, of being in a shining lacquer sheath. When open, the spokes, which in fact are the only part to have been lacquered, make the umbrella glisten like a shining wheel, emphasizing the structure, and framing the simple but rich colours of the overall design. Small wonder that to the foreign mind the Japanese paper umbrella has become one of the symbols of picturesque Japan.

筆
瞕

Craft and
Language

8

Writing and Painting Brushes *Fude*

In Japan, following the tradition of Chinese aesthetics, painting and calligraphy are closely related. There is no clear-cut distinction between a painting and a writing brush and most brushes can equally well be used by the painter or the calligrapher. The range of brushes is enormous. The finest brushes may have only a few hairs, while at the other end of the scale there are brushes whose head alone may be 25 cm (9·8 in.) wide or more, and must be wielded with two hands. Prices are equally various, ranging from a few hundred yen to thousands. But whatever the size and whatever the price, owners treat their brushes, and all their writing implements, with a deep respect and a special affection. Over the centuries great artistry has been lavished on writing boxes, ink stones, water droppers and all the equipment of the calligrapher, and the finest brushes are highly-prized possessions.

Early tomb paintings suggest that the Japanese may have had simple painting brushes before the Buddhist era, but it was with the introduction of Buddhism and Chinese culture around the sixth century AD that the true writing brush came to Japan. Up to that time, amazing as it may seem, the Japanese had no written language and so the Chinese characters were taken over and 'fitted' to the existing Japanese spoken language. This marriage was made easier by the addition of two supplementary phonetic sets of characters, the *kanas*, but still today Japanese writing is basically made up of thousands of Chinese characters called *kanji*. In practice this means that while Japanese and Chinese cannot understand each other's spoken language, they can roughly communicate in writing.

With Chinese writing, and Chinese black-ink painting, came the tapered Chinese writing brush, essential for the fine writing of Chinese characters. This type of brush still remains central to Japanese life. The oldest brushes in Japan are those in the Shōsōin at Nara, the Emperor Shomu's treasure of the eighth century, which has been perfectly preserved; in a sense the oldest museum in the world. These brushes are made of rabbit, racoon and other animal furs and range in length from 30 to 65 cm (11·8–25·6 in.). They were brought from China. In the early ninth century Kukai, the famous priest who founded the Shingon sect, returned from China and ordered brushes to be made in Japan following Chinese methods. These are said to have been the first Japanese brushes.

In those early days the craft of brush-making was controlled by the Imperial Court and there was an Imperial office for this purpose. But by the middle of the Heian period more and more people outside court circles needed writing brushes and the craft passed into private hands, with a rapidly increasing number of craftsmen.

During the Edo period, with the Tokugawa government's adoption of Confucian principles, 'the Chinese style' in many things enjoyed great popularity, and as part of this the 'roll brush' was replaced by the Chinese 'water brush', made of hair from the horse or deer. The roll brush had its hairs built around a solid core which meant that only the tip could be used. The water brush is made entirely of hair, and the whole of the head of the brush not only holds the ink but can be used in writing or painting which makes it more suitable for both writing and painting in the Chinese style. This brush allows a much greater variety of strokes and more variety and subtlety in shading, essential if you remember that in Chinese ink painting there are five 'colours' of black! After the Edo period there were no further changes and brush-making has remained one of Japan's most traditional crafts. The brush described in the craft section of this chapter is the standard water brush in use today.

The hair of sheep, horse and deer are most commonly used for brushes, but on occasion the hair of other animals is used, either alone or in a mixture. Brushes can be made from Japanese goat, badger, cat and rabbit hair, or weasel hair from Russia; the horse hair comes from America and the sheep and deer hair from China. The hair from some of these animals is taken from more than one part of the body. With the horse, for example, hair is taken from the belly, the tail and around the hooves. Under a microscope the hairs of different animals can be seen to have slightly different shapes. These contribute to the character of a particular brush.

The head of the brush can either be mounted directly into the bamboo handle, or there can be a separate mount joining the brush head to the handle. Some brushes are mounted in buffalo horn or ivory, while today black and white plastic are commonly used. Some high-quality brushes are mounted in rare bamboos from China, though normally a bamboo from Shikoku is used. The handles of brushes can also be made of woods other than bamboo.

For calligraphy, and black-ink painting, *sumi* or traditional Chinese ink is used. The best ink in Japan is made around Nara, as are many fine writing brushes. The ink is made from soot made by burning rapeseed oil; this is mixed with animal glue and perfume and formed into highly decorated small blocks or sticks. To obtain the desired consistency of *sumi*, the sticks are rubbed with water on an ink stone. A good brush will absorb and hold the ink well, and give an even flow in use.

Tremendous control is required in writing elaborate Chinese characters which can have as many as forty separate strokes, and fine writing must depend on a fine brush. There are of course many styles of calligraphy, ranging from the carefully controlled classic Chinese styles through to the wild, ink-splattering styles of the great Zen calligraphers where sometimes one feels that the brush has been hurled at the paper from across the room, and maybe on occasion it was. It is difficult for the Westerner to appreciate

Seal-Engraving
Plate 18 Three seals, their sides decorated in the typical style of Clifton Karhu
Plate 19 A selection of seals, all designed and cut by Karhu. (See Chapter Nine)

the finer points of Japanese calligraphy. I remember once making a long detour to visit a private museum famous for its Japanese ceramics. On arrival I was disappointed to find that for that month all the exquisite tea ceremony pieces had been put back into store to make room for an exhibition of the museum's fine collection of calligraphy. I wandered around and in my limited way enjoyed some of the large and spectacular masterpieces, but when I came to the prize piece displayed alone in a case in the centre of the room, I was lost. It was a poem written on a small piece of paper by an early Japanese emperor. In my abysmal ignorance I would have passed it by as little more exciting than a rapidly scrawled laundry list!

Of course, the Chinese characters or *kanji* are by their very nature both beautiful and fascinating, and like the language they represent, they lie at the heart of Japanese culture. Calligraphy has become an art separated from daily life and today only a comparatively few Japanese write *kanji* well with a brush. On certain occasions every Japanese is required to write with a brush, recording their names at weddings and funerals or similar formal occasions, but mostly today *kanji* is written with a ballpoint pen or other modern instrument. Since the Second World War Japanese have needed to know some two thousand characters, though many people know more. The burden of learning so many characters is a heavy one and takes up a large part of Japanese schooling between the ages of eight and twelve. There is little doubt that the Japanese have the deepest feelings about their written language and seem prepared to put up with the time, effort and inconvenience its learning and use involves.

The Chinese, who after all invented the characters, are making moves to simplify their written language. For many years there has been some debate in Japan about the possibility of doing the same thing but, with their innate conservatism, most Japanese feel that the loss of *kanji* could undermine the whole of Japanese life and culture. It is an interesting debate with good arguments on both sides. I sometimes feel that the innate Japanese gift for design and a widespread manual dexterity may have something to do with that hard discipline of mastering *kanji*; there can be little doubt that it must also be connected with the excellent memories most Japanese students seem blessed with. On the other hand, *kanji* exacts a heavy price in the educational system which might partly explain why the Japanese today are the most literate nation, but not necessarily the best-educated.

Making a Brush

Nara, one of Japan's earliest capitals, is famous for its painting and writing brushes. We were privileged to be allowed to make this study at the well-

56

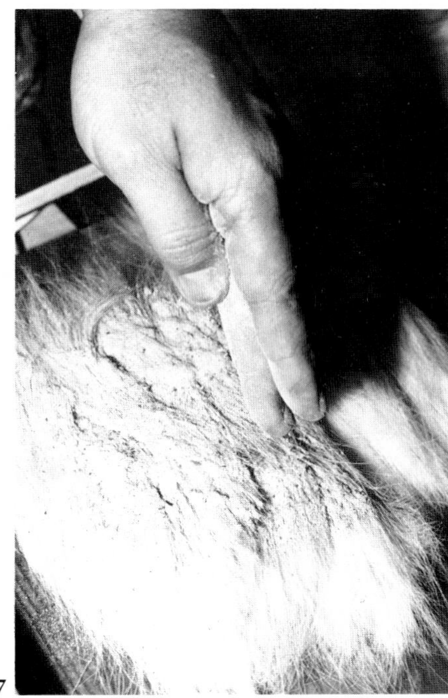

57

56 The right grade of hair is chosen for the particular brush

57 The hair is sprinkled with ash

known shop and workshop, Hakubundo, just south of Nara, and owned by the Kusaka family. It was founded in 1878. Kiyokazu Otuji-san, who showed us all the processes involved in making a brush, is one of the most highly regarded brushmakers of the area and has been making brushes for over thirty years. His long experience was obvious from the dextrous and rapid way he handled and sorted the wool of the sheep he was working with for this brush.

First, exactly the right grade of hair must be chosen for the kind of brush being made. The hair must be from the right animal, from the right part of that animal, and of the correct thickness and length. We were shown a magnificent brush for calligraphy worth over 750,000 yen, the hair for which had been minutely picked out from 10 kg (22 lb) of wool. The selection alone took two days. After the hair has been chosen, it is cleaned and sterilized in boiling water, and the roots of the hair are then combed to remove any skin, follicle cells or any other matter still attached to the roots.

Next, ash made from rice husks is sprinkled over the hair and an electric heating board is placed over the top. Any remaining oil is absorbed by the ash, and the heat dries the hair. The hairs are then rubbed together in a chamois leather to straighten them, and afterwards untangled by further patient combing. Then, the straightened hairs are plucked and sorted so that they are all the right way up. They are made into a small bundle by tapping one end against a small board, and then any loose hairs are trimmed carefully with a knife.

Incense
Plate 20 A box of attractively wrapped sticks of incense
Plate 21 Cones of incense traditionally wrapped for export. (See Chapter Ten)

ORIGINAL TEMPLE INCENSE
CONTENTS 18 PCS. SHOYEIDO & CO., LTD. KYOTO JAPAN

58 Having been rolled in a chamois leather, the straightened hairs are sorted

Now the hairs must be cut into five different lengths so that when mixed together they will give the brush a tapered shape. The hair is dampened with water and, using five small wooden gauges, it is cut into five different lengths with scissors. These lengths will vary depending on the size of the brush being made. The craftsman now has five piles of hair which must be thoroughly mixed together. Using only one quarter of the pile at a time, the lengths are layered one on top of the other, the longest hair on the bottom, the shortest on the top. This pile of five lengths is rolled and combed, then flattened out, re-rolled and combed again. The process is repeated about five times until the craftsman is satisfied that the different lengths are thoroughly mixed together.

This bundle of mixed lengths of hair is now covered with starch paste and divided up to make a number of brushes, the number depending on the amount of hair required for the size of brushes being made. Each of these brushes is now held together by slipping a small black plastic collar along its length to the base. The collar simply secures the hairs while the brush is dried for one day.

The brush is then rolled inside a wet 'sheet' of fine-quality hair which makes an outer casing. This is for appearance: it is the body of the brush that will do the work. The brush is now tied tightly at the base with two loops of

59 The five different lengths of hair

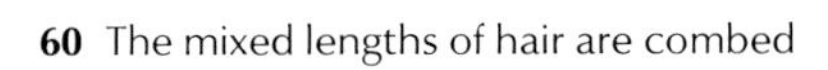

60 The mixed lengths of hair are combed

Overleaf
Incense
Plate 22 Small silk bags containing powdered incense. (See Chapter Ten)

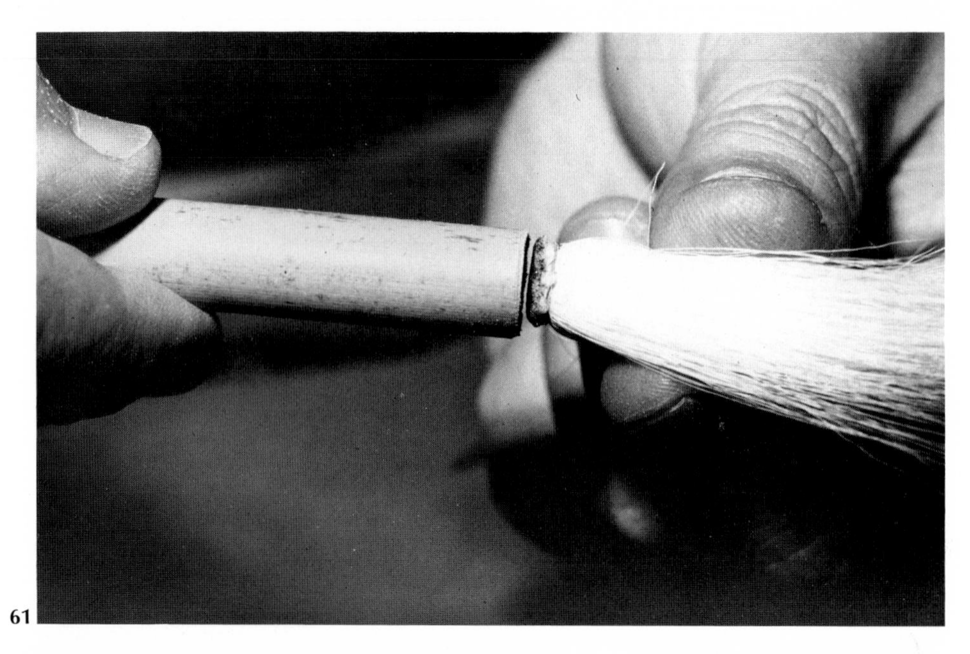

61 The brush is fitted into the handle

hemp string, and the end pressed against a hot iron which melts the hair as if it were plastic and bonds it together.

If the brush is to be fitted directly into a bamboo handle, the top of the bamboo is hollowed out with a knife to make a hole of exactly the right size to receive the brush. Some glue is put inside the hole and the end of the brush is pressed firmly into place.

Now the brush must be shaped. First a bundle of brushes is thoroughly rubbed in thick starch paste. Then the excess paste is squeezed and combed out, and the final shape is given to the brush by drawing it through a tight loop of string, which also ensures an even distribution of the remaining paste along the length of the brush. The craftsman finishes the shaping by hand and the brushes are then left to dry for a day or so. Finally, the name of the shop, and on better-quality brushes the seal of the craftsman, are added to the handles of the finished brushes.

Practical Note

Although many people in the West are now using Japanese brushes, one cannot recommend this craft even to the most gifted Western craftsman. Taken individually, the processes may appear simple, but in fact the choice of the correct strands of hair and the handling of them during the making of the brush require not only a teacher, but a judgment and skill based on years of practice. It is perhaps partly the enormous skill that goes into making a brush that makes them almost revered by their Japanese owners.

62 Some finished brushes, mounted in black plastic. The handles are marked with the maker's name

62

Paper Lanterns
Plate 23 The cane skeleton of a paper lantern
Plate 24 Decorative Chinese characters are painted on to a large paper lantern. (See Chapter Eleven)

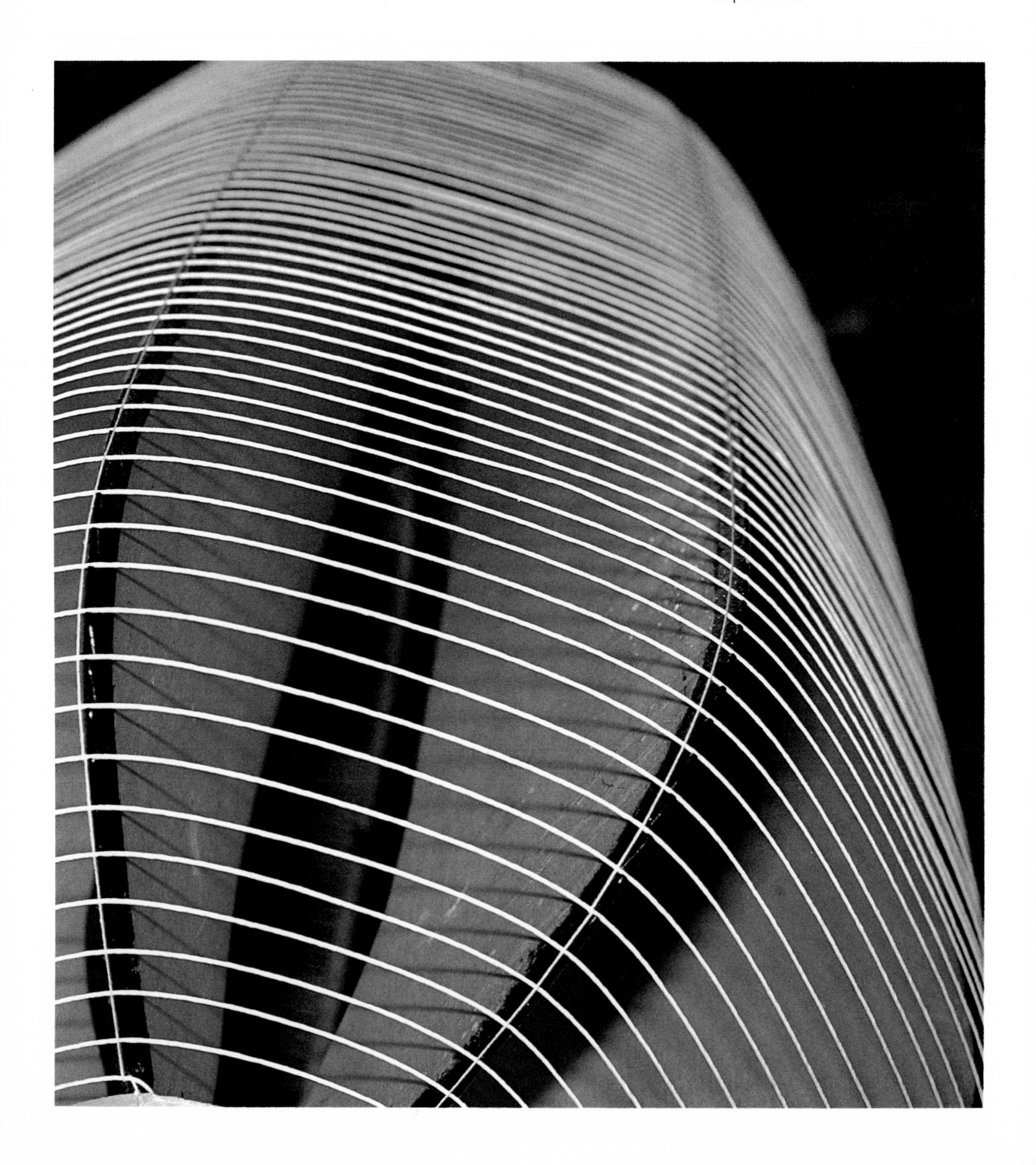

町
氏子中

9

Seal-Engraving
Tenkoku

In Japan today – where robots build cars, where eighty per cent of your banking is done through a machine, where the humblest coffee shop has automatic doors and where the arrival of express trains gives you the time to the nearest five seconds – no Japanese can exist without two personal seals engraved with their name, a system nearly thirteen hundred years old.

The written signature is not legally valid in Japan. Each Japanese carries an everyday seal for such things as receipts and delivery notes, and they also have a formal and officially registered seal for signing important documents. Foreigners are allowed to register a seal, but it has to be written, not in Chinese characters, but in *katakana*, the phonetic alphabet used mainly for writing foreign words. Forging another person's seal is an extremely serious offence. It is easy enough to obtain the everyday seal as they are for sale everywhere, engraved with all the commoner Japanese family names. Once, when a Japanese friend was unable to be present at the signing of my lease, for which he was guarantor, he gave me permission to buy a cheap seal engraved with his name and seal the lease in his absence. The world of *tenkoku* is a good example of that bewildering mixture of ancient and modern which is Japan.

The Japanese learned the use of seals from the Chinese and the system was legalized in Japan in AD 701 when everyone at court had their own official seal. These seals were made by the government and were only used on official documents. About the middle of the eighth century nobles who served the Emperor were allowed personal seals, and in 770 the twelve main Buddhist temples of Nara, the then capital, were also given seals. But it was not until the seventeenth and eighteenth centuries that the use of seals became more general. In the Meiji period, laws were introduced controlling the use of official seals. Each government department had a variety of seals, each for use with certain kinds of documents, a practice which still continues.

Personal seals are usually 1 to 1·5 cm (0·4–0·6 in.) in width, and the face is made in a variety of shapes, most commonly square, circular or elliptical. The everyday seal, now mass-produced by machine, may be carried in a small case fitted with an ink pad. If a Japanese has no seal available, their thumb print is legally acceptable.

Based on Chinese tradition, the seal is always made with red ink, though the tone varies. The art of seal-engraving is the contrast of red and white. Red is an auspicious colour, suitable for celebration. In Japan rice is coloured red for festive occasions, while gifts to mark happy events should be tied with red and white ribbons. Two distinct types of ink are used with seals. Modern seals are often pressed against a pad impregnated with a liquid red ink. But for the traditional seal, to produce a rich impression, an extremely thick ink is used, usually kept in a ceramic box. This ink is almost solid but contains oil to stop it drying out. It is expensive as it contains gold which adds richness to its colour. Use of this thick ink clogs up the face of the seal which must be cleaned with a small brush and washed.

Seals are made from a variety of materials and come in a variety of shapes and sizes, though they must be large enough to allow a firm grip to achieve a good impression. Wood is popular, particularly for cheaper seals, and plum, cherry, torreya, blackwood and boxwood are all suitable. While Japanese woodblocks for prints are engraved on the cross-grain, wooden seals are engraved on the curly grain. More valuable materials include certain precious stones, agate, crystal, ivory, ceramics, rhinoceros horn, and softer stones such as soapstone. But however precious the material and however beautiful the design of the seal, its true worth will lie in the quality of the engraver's work, in the design and cutting of the characters, a craft of intricate specialization, like so many things in Japan.

The following experience not only highlights that degree of specialization, but shows something of the ethos surrounding well-known Japanese craftsmen. Some years ago I thought of having a seal cut of the sort used by Japanese book collectors; their version of our bookplate. I was lunching in Tokyo with a friend who is a particular expert on traditional Japanese crafts and I asked her advice. She explained the many different kinds of seal and the fact that craftsmen specialized in engraving one particular kind. With all the blundering enthusiasm of a foreigner I asked if we could go that afternoon to visit a seal-engraver specializing in book collectors' seals. With well-concealed exasperation my friend gently explained that that was impossible. First, the only two good seal-engravers of that kind worked in Kyoto, and second, third and fourth, commissioning a seal was not done in one afternoon! She explained the procedure.

It was fortunate, she said, that I was going to live in Kyoto shortly. Once settled there and having decided whose style I preferred, I should obtain an introduction to that seal-engraver and for some months thereafter, without mentioning the commission, I should call regularly to study his work and to give him the opportunity to study me. When I felt that some rapport had been established, then I might most tentatively mention the possibility of commissioning a seal. Now that I had prepared the ground so carefully, the answer could well be 'yes', but I should also be prepared to receive a polite refusal.

Regretfully, this was all too daunting and I never tried to commission a seal. There was a practical obstacle too. I realized that Japanese seal ink would not take on many of the unabsorbent papers used in modern and Western books. However, I learned a number of lessons from my friend's advice which I have found useful on other Japanese occasions. In Japan one must learn to 'hasten slowly'.

What I am going to write now to some extent contradicts what I have already written. This is the only craft in this book where we based our study on the work of a non-Japanese artist and craftsman who has mastered a Japanese craft, to the point where his seals are eagerly sought after by Japanese collectors. I have included this one Western craftsman to demonstrate that Japanese crafts are not beyond the skill of Western hands or the understanding of a Western mind and heart. Such a thing is not easily achieved, not least because so many Japanese think it impossible, but with time and determination a few foreigners succeed.

There are a number of talented foreign artists working in Japan, but to me Clifton Karhu is the most gifted and most versatile, and probably best-known among Japanese. He is an American of Finnish origin and much about him speaks of this mixture. He first came to Japan in 1947 as a Christian missionary. Through Japan, through his study of the language, and through learning to paint in the Japanese style, one might say that 'he heard new voices'. Although he always wears kimono ('I like to remind the Japanese of the good things they are giving up') and his work is deeply Japanese in character, both the American and the Finn are still there, sustaining a simple directness amidst the asymmetric workings of the Japanese world in which he moves so freely.

Like many gifted artists, Clif Karhu is extremely prolific and amazingly versatile. His reputation as a major artist in Japan is founded on some twenty years as a woodblock-print artist, mainly of Kyoto architecture and landscapes. He has had many exhibitions of prints, which he can cut and print himself. In turn the prints have been adapted as designs for kimono, *furoshiki* and other things, while many prints have been commissioned for restaurant calendars, saké bottle labels and other forms of advertising.

For several years Clif Karhu has also been painting in the Japanese style in black ink (*sumi-e*), with charming illustrations of Japanese proverbs, and other subjects. Many of these show his warm humour, seen at its best in his Zen painting, which is a remarkable example of his intuitive understanding of something so essentially Japanese.

Clif Karhu says that seals were the first form of Japanese art he fell in love with, shortly after his arrival. This became associated with his interest in Chinese characters (*kanji*) and calligraphy. His style of seal-engraving is very much his own, just as are the humorous themes with which he decorates their sides. They are based on Japanese techniques, but he never allows rigid rules to inhibit his spirit. Those rules may be essential to Japanese craftsmen. Breaking them, or more often gently bending them, gives Clif Karhu an added stimulation.

There are the gravest dangers for Western artists working in or near the Japanese idiom. Somehow Clif Karhu succeeds in balancing on this

63 Clifton Karhu engraving a seal in his studio in Kyoto

63

tightrope stretched between East and West. Sometimes, as with his prints, he inclines to the West; at others, as with his ink painting, he leans sharply towards the East. But whatever the results, the work has an integrity and originality that is not quite East or West – it is Karhu!

Engraving a Seal

Karhu's design and technique in seal-engraving are based on Japanese tradition but, as in all his work, he adapts that tradition to suit his own style. The seal he designed, engraved and decorated for this study is typical of his work and was later included in an exhibition in Nagoya, though usually he only makes seals to order.

Like any work of art, the success of a seal, however skilfully cut, will depend on its design. Traditional Japanese seal-engravers follow formal rules of composition which aim at achieving strength, elegance and harmony, largely through a correct relationship between the *kanji* characters and the space and frame that enclose them. Karhu recognizes and respects these principles, but composes his design in a freer style. The success of the design will also partly depend on the choice of suitable characters where the seal includes more than just a person's name. The characters must be harmoniously balanced both in appearance and meaning. With thousands of characters to choose from, the permutations are bewildering. Karhu has a considerable knowledge of *kanji* which fascinates him by its beauty, variety and flexibility.

Karhu draws the chosen characters with a brush and black ink on a strip of paper, composing them in the shape of the seal face. He then considers the spacing of the characters, and drawing the shape of the seal, marks off the spaces before painting in the characters.

The characters must be engraved in reverse on the seal to appear the right way round in the impression. There are two ways of doing this. For the less experienced, the design can be painted on thin paper which is then reversed and this image copied. Karhu sometimes does this but more usually simply paints the characters in reverse directly on to the face of the seal.

Seal-engravers buy ready-made seal blanks, choosing a particular shape and material for a particular commission or design. In this instance Karhu was using a block of a type of soapstone. Seals can vary greatly in size, though personal seals are seldom large. Karhu makes seals only 1 to 2 cm (0·4–0·8 in.) wide, and others 7 cm (2·7 in.) and more. He seems to prefer square seals. Before engraving the blank, Karhu makes certain that its face is absolutely level, ensuring a perfect impression. He paints the face with red

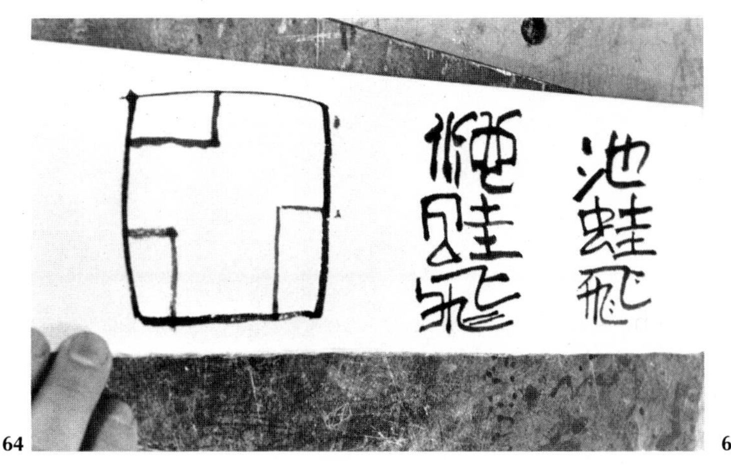

64

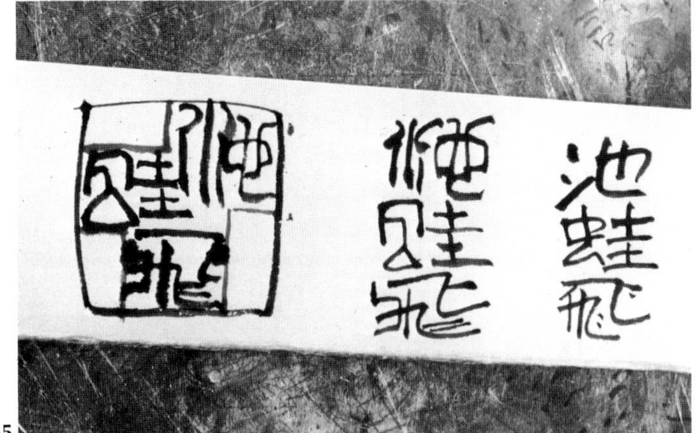

65

64 The characters are first painted on paper in the rough shape of the seal, and alongside the spaces between the characters are roughed out

65 The characters are then painted into the spaces

66 The characters are painted in black ink on to the red face of the seal

67 The characters are engraved in low relief

66

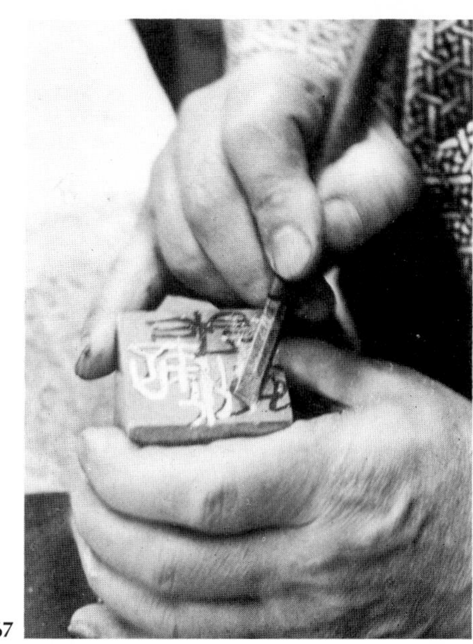

67

ink and, working on a flat surface, rubs the face on a sheet of sandpaper until he has removed all the ink.

Next, he again paints the level face with red ink, to make a clear background on which to paint in black and cut the characters. These are now painted on with a brush in black ink and when the ink is dry he is ready to start cutting. Some Japanese engravers hold the seal in a small wooden clamp. Karhu prefers to hold it in his hand, resting it on a soft pad of folded cloth. He then selects a suitable chisel, which he sharpens on a wet stone. He holds his chisels like a Western pen, but many Japanese engravers hold the chisel with the end pointing away from them.

The characters can either be cut in high relief (male), or in low relief (female). This seal was cut in low relief. Using red ink, the male seal will

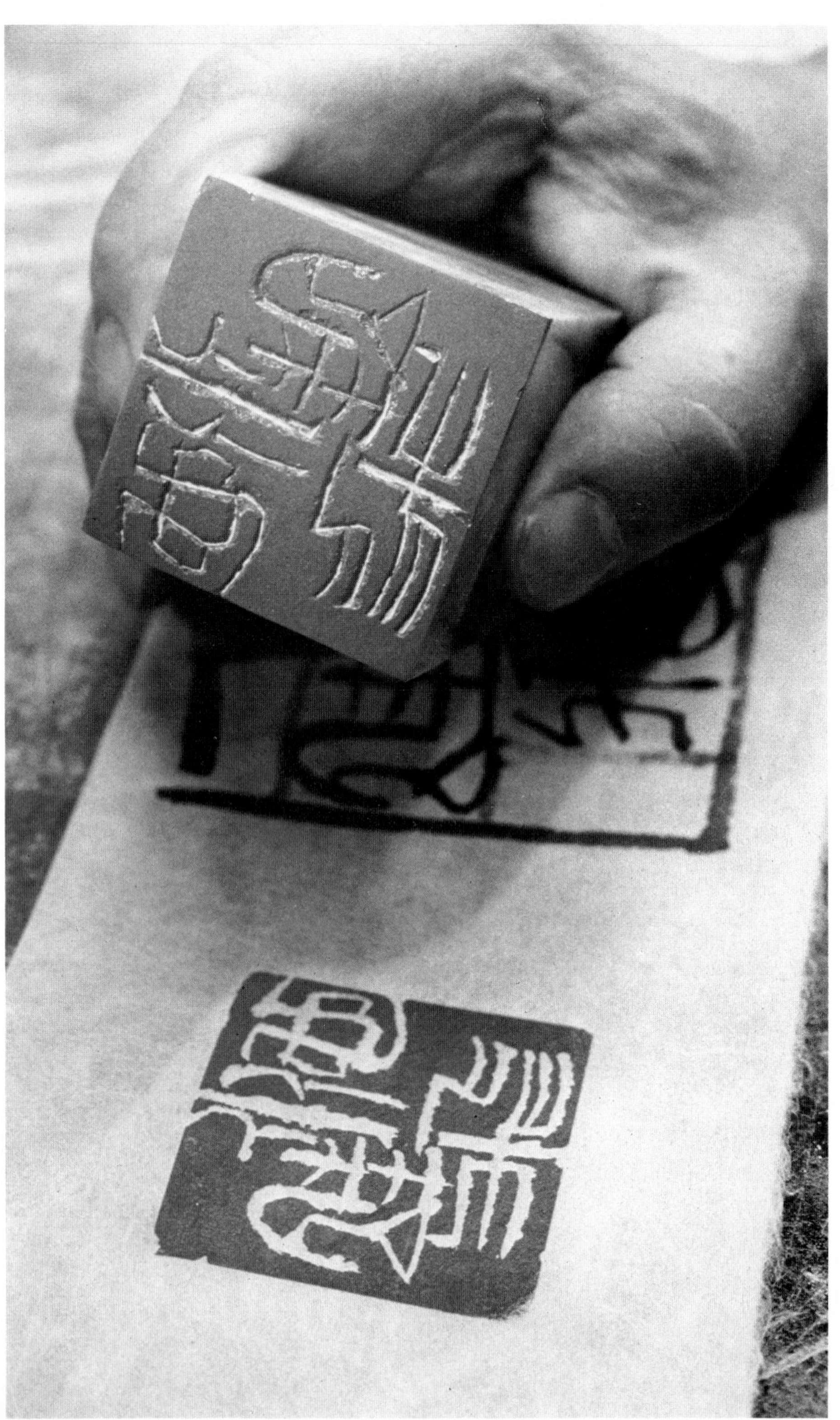

68 The engraved face of the seal and the impression on paper with red ink. As it is a female seal the characters print in white

produce red characters on a white ground; the female seal white characters on a red ground. Unexpectedly, low-relief characters are said to be harder to cut than high-relief characters. The correct use of red and white characters, or the right contrast in a mixed seal, is vital in traditional seal design.

When the engraving is finished, the face is cleaned of any remaining red ink, and the engraving carefully checked before any impression is made. Now the seal is pressed into the thick red ink. Normally the ink container is larger than the seal face but on this occasion Karhu had to use a small circular box of ink and therefore had to ink the seal corner by corner. It is not easy to get an even spread of ink or to apply the correct pressure.

The seal is now firmly pressed down on a piece of Japanese paper whose absorbency will take a good impression. Now the seal and paper are turned upwards. The back of the paper is gently rubbed with a pad called a *baren*, to ensure a perfect impression. The pad, also used in taking impressions of woodblock prints, is a circular mat of finely woven bamboo covered with a bamboo leaf. Its slightly uneven surface forces the ink into the deepest crevices of the engraving. In the old days, when the slightly rough surface of *tatami* matting covered every floor, that would have provided a perfect rubbing surface, the *baren* simply acting as a substitute. The seal is now lifted off the paper and the impression carefully checked. At this late stage, using a fine chisel, it is simple to make slight alterations. The face of the seal is now finished and the seal ready for decoration.

69 The finished engraving. Note how the careful positioning of the frog's legs emphasizes the three-dimensional quality of its head

69

The practice of decorating the sides of seals has precedents in China where seals were engraved with landscapes, but traditionally in Japan the decoration of seals is usually limited to carving a small animal on the top. Karhu's engraved seal decoration is highly individual, often humorous and, in personal commissions, the subject may be related in some way to the name or nature of the patron. Karhu once made a set of seals for me and encircled them with a splendid sprawling dragon. This referred to the fact that under the oriental zodiac I was born in the Year of the Dragon, and was also a play on my name which, given a Japanese pronunciation, means 'dragon'. The characters on the seals also pursued this 'dragon theme'.

Having decided the design for the decoration, which often comes directly out of his fertile imagination, Karhu paints it directly on to the sides of the seal in black ink. Like the frog here, these designs often run around all four sides in an unbroken design, a highly creative and lateral form of thinking. A variety of suitable chisels is then used to engrave the design in low relief.

When the carving is finished, the whole design is painted over with black ink which is carefully brushed into the depths of the engraving. When the ink is dry, it is lightly wiped off with a moist cloth, leaving the engraved design picked out in black against the background of the greenish stone. Karhu finally engraves his signature on one side of the seal.

70 A variety of seals designed by Clifton Karhu

Practical Note

Both the materials and techniques involved in cutting a seal are simple. And it is hoped that Karhu's relaxed approach and free style will encourage others to try this craft. Materials and suitable chisels should be easily available anywhere. Japanese inks and papers are now for sale around the world.

The fact that you cannot read the Chinese characters need not deter you from using them. As design motifs they are beautiful in themselves, and it is easy to buy a small Japanese dictionary. I have known beautiful calligraphy done by Westerners who could not understand a single character. And who knows? Maybe like Clif Karhu, initial fascination with the intrinsic design may lead to a knowledge of the written language. Karhu also sometimes cuts seals using the Roman alphabet so there are no excuses, even for the less adventurous.

香榭

Ritual

10

Incense
Ko

Incense came to Japan with Buddhism in the middle of the sixth century AD, and has remained an important part of Buddhist ritual. Millions of sticks of incense are still burned every day in the temples and before the family altars of Japan. In early times incense was mainly used in temples, burned before the Buddhist statues or by the memorial tablets of the dead. In Buddhism incense is basically a symbol of purification. From about the eighth century the religious idea was transferred to secular life when the Heian nobility began scenting their rooms and clothes with incense; a practice that has continued until today.

This aristocratic interest in the variety of incenses developed into a competition with an elaborate ceremony called *kōdō*. The ceremony seems to have developed during the Muromachi period, but its exact origins are obscure. Using beautiful equipment, the host burned different kinds of incense which his guests tried to identify. Since some two hundred kinds were available, a discerning sense of smell was required. About the same time the use of incense spread and even warriors scented their armour. People put incense in beautiful small silk bags which they tucked inside their kimonos or sashes, or hung in their rooms. Scented bags are still produced in huge quantities, but Western scents have become more fashionable in recent years.

In every popular Buddhist temple a large incense burner stands before the main hall. This great bronze bowl is full of smouldering charcoal. To one side temple stalls sell amulets, souvenirs and bundles of incense sticks wrapped in brightly coloured paper. The bundle is lit from those already burning and stood upright in the charcoal ash. As the sweet smoke rises the person draws it over themselves with their hand. This may be a symbolic act of purification, but many people believe in the healing powers of incense and draw the smoke to some affected part of their body. Inside the temple, incense is offered to statues of the Buddha or burned as part of the ritual of a service. Among the esoteric sects of Buddhism, each uses a different kind of incense.

Many Japanese homes still have a family altar to honour their ancestors, where incense is burned on memorial occasions. I remember once having supper with a Japanese family in Nagoya. Just before the meal I sensed that I was the cause of some distress to the very old grandmother. My much younger hostess explained that always before the evening meal her grandmother liked to offer food and incense in memory of her husband at the *butsudan*, but was embarrassed by the presence of a foreigner. I can still picture the look of relief on the old lady's face when I asked permission to join her.

We made our study of incense at the famous Kyoto shop, Shoeido, founded nearly two hundred and eighty years ago. Today it is run by the eleventh generation of the family, Shigetaro Hata-san. It was a special privilege to be allowed behind the scenes of such a venerable establishment, and Hata-san and his staff were most helpful in explaining the types of incense and their numerous ingredients.

Apart from some chemical ingredients which have crept into the making of incense, the materials come from a few animals, and a wide variety of trees and plants, in the form of bark, leaves, wood or roots. Some incense, including the most expensive, is simply flakes of a rare wood burnt on charcoal. Other incenses are made up of several ingredients, bound together with oil and water.

Animal materials include dried whale meat and the dried lymph gland of the Tibetan male Jakko deer (the latter now so scarce that the tiny bag we were shown was worth 875,000 yen). I remember being given a lunch in Kyoto by a group of Japanese students I had taught in England. They presented me with a handsome box and inside, mostly carefully wrapped, was a piece of tree root, about 6 cm (2·3 in.) long, from a rare Chinese tree and one of the most admired forms of incense in Japan. I realized it was a very special gift, but was dismayed when that very afternoon I saw in a shop that my fragment of sweet-burning root cost some 25,000 yen. Materials come from afar: cloves from Zanzibar, a shell from Madagascar and many plants and fragrant woods from China and South-East Asia. It is an exotic trade handled by the Chinese merchants of Hong Kong and Singapore.

Incense is made in four main forms in Japan. The sticks described in the craft section of this chapter are now the commonest, burned singly or in bundles. They were introduced from China in the late seventeenth century by a Chinaman who later took Japanese nationality. Up to that time the incense shops had largely depended for their trade on the incense ceremony and welcomed this new idea to expand their business.

Incense is also sometimes used within the ritual of the tea ceremony and for this must be of the highest quality. In winter only, the season they are used, small pellets are made by kneading together powdered woods and animal materials with honey or Japanese apricot. At the tea ceremony these pellets are contained in beautifully designed, small incense boxes and are burned in equally beautiful burners, all according to an elaborate ritual.

Special types of incense are prepared for the incense ceremony or game, mostly whole materials such as flakes of rare woods. For the small bags tucked into the kimono, a dry powdered incense is used which gives off its scent without heat. Bamboo baskets are made specially to hold several bags which are hung from the ceiling. In storing clothes sweetly perfumed sachets were tucked in the folds, partly a protection against moth. These can still be bought but it sometimes seems that the moths find the smell as attractive as oneself!

71 The dry, ground ingredients are mixed together

Incense is one of those elements of Japanese life that remind one of the importance of ritual. It is sometimes said that the Japanese are more ritualistic than religious, and in a Western sense that is probably true. Worship in Japan, Shinto or Buddhist, seems to an observer of the Christian tradition to be largely a matter of form. The pilgrim who may have saved for years to visit the Shinto Grand Shrine at Ise, once arrived at the sanctuary pauses only a few seconds to clap hands and bow before turning back. However, to the Japanese those few seconds are perhaps as meaningful as several emotional hours prostrate before the shrine at Lourdes in France.

In Japan one may apologize by bowing low or, if a gangster, by cutting off a finger. Both acts take about the same time, and both are rituals. Until there is some means of measuring the amount of feeling involved in a ritual, one should be careful of dismissing any act as merely ritualistic.

Making Sticks of Incense

It might seem surprising that Shoeido, founded in 1705, and one of the most famous makers of incense in Japan, should make such great use of modern machinery in their production. However, economic pressures have forced many traditional craftsmen to install some machinery and to adopt some modern and more efficient materials. Since in nearly all cases, and certainly in the case of incense, this modernization has had little effect on the quality or the appearance of the product, it is a sensible development which helps to ensure that the general public can still afford these traditional crafts.

72 A cylindrical cake of incense is removed from the compressor

In the previous section it was explained that Japanese incense comes in various forms but here we can only describe one kind of incense made by Shoeido, the incense stick. These are burned daily in thousands of temples throughout Japan. It is the most common form of incense and the one that plays the most important part in modern Japanese life. With such a widespread use, it is not surprising that today incense sticks are mass-produced by modern machinery.

Unlike Indian incense sticks which have a central bamboo support, Japanese sticks are wholly made of incense and, though extremely thin, can be burned singly as well as in bundles. Their rigidity comes from the materials used which include powdered wood and plant material, and both natural and chemical perfumes, drawn from the materials already described. In the first stage the ingredients of a particular recipe are mixed together dry, and this mixture is passed through an electrically-vibrated sieve to ensure that all the grains are of equal size.

This sieved material is then put into a machine that both rolls and mixes. Hot water is added which contains the chemical dye to colour the sticks red, yellow, blue or green. During the kneading of the mixture by the heavy rollers in this machine, perfumed oil is added. After about twenty minutes the consistency is checked and, if too moist, more powder is added. If the consistency is correct, large lumps of the incense are now placed in a cylindrical compressor and the lump is pressed into the cylindrical shape required by the next process.

These blocks of incense are now placed in a different compressor which, by squeezing the block at the top, forces it out through small holes in the

73 As the threads of incense are extruded by the second compressor, they are collected on a wooden board

74 The dried sticks of incense are sorted into equal bundles with a measuring rod

base-plate of the machine in threads about the size of vermicelli. The operator sits and collects the threads on wooden boards. These boards are taken by another man who carefully transfers the threads on to long aluminium trays. The width of these is exactly the required length of the finished sticks, making it simple to trim the threads. These trays are placed in an oven for two hours to dry the incense sticks. When removed from the oven and cooled, they are rigid enough for handling.

The sticks must now be boxed individually, or made up into bundles. Girls, working directly from the aluminium trays, 'count' the correct number of sticks for each bundle by the simple means of measuring the necessary length of sticks with a bamboo rod, and separating each bundle-length. Then the bundles are hand-wrapped in bright papers and labels of handsome traditional design which suggest a more exotic method of production than the rather mundane factory process described above.

75

75 Bundles of sticks are wrapped in brightly coloured and decorated bundles

Practical Note

From the processes described in this chapter, it is obvious that neither materials or manufacture offer much encouragement to the do-it-yourself enthusiast. But remember that the most admired and most precious Japanese incenses are nothing more than burning flakes of rare fragrant woods. In the West, the special fragrance of certain woods, particularly fruitwoods, is recognized where open fires still exist. Experiments could be made with local woods and plants, and possibly a local version of the incense game devised. It must have been by such experiments, or even accidents, that the fragrant materials of the East were discovered. But please, one word of warning. A contemporary of mine at Oxford set his room on fire by falling asleep having lit a soporific stick of incense!

Overleaf
Paper Lanterns
Plate 25 Everywhere in Japan, long rows of paper lanterns decorate the buildings. (See Chapter Eleven)

めんるい
丼物一式
東山八坂
電561五一九八八番
東山線京都神社道角
電代561一三〇一〇八五四番

大阪ガス代理店
営業用器具ショップ

下弁天町
平井卯三郎

11

Paper Lanterns *Chōchin*

The Japanese paper lantern has long been part of the picturesque image of Japan. They are still a charming feature of Japanese life, hung row upon row in Shinto shrines and Buddhist temples, or individually as a form of sign or advertisement outside the more traditional shops and restaurants. Kyoto remains a city of lanterns which on a summer evening spread their soft glow everywhere. Now largely decorative, for centuries the paper lantern was a practical form of lighting, if not very powerful, the fixed lanterns lighting their immediate area, and smaller hand-held lanterns lighting the traveller's path.

The folding paper lantern seems to have come to Japan from China probably as late as the sixteenth century. Japan had long had large stone and metal lanterns and simpler forms of domestic lighting. But the first paper-covered lantern appeared about 1570, a type already used in Ming China. This was not a folding lantern but a rigid cylinder of bamboo basketwork, papered over, with a carrying handle at the top and the candle fixed to a baseboard. This was the basket lantern (*kago chōtin*), and this earliest type remained in use in Northern Japan until recent times.

The first Japanese folding lantern was the box lantern (*hako chōtin*), the classic design of paper lantern of plain cylindrical form with a circular wooden cap and base. This may also have come from China but its origin is uncertain. It appeared in Japan about 1590. After this time, during the Edo period, paper lanterns came into general use and a variety of designs were developed, each for a special purpose or occasion.

The box lantern was slightly altered over the years. Originally the top and bottom parts of this lantern were made from the twisted tendrils of wistaria, used for many things in Japan from the handles of bamboo baskets for flower arrangement to special kinds of painting brushes. Later the ends of the lantern were made of thin bent wood which was lacquered black and fitted at the top with a handle. Originally, this type of lantern was used for various purposes but later its use became more ceremonial until finally it became the lantern for welcoming and bidding farewell to guests in the red-light districts.

A thinner, more elongated version of the box lantern, called *Odawara chōtin* (Odawara is a famous town, gateway to the Hakone/Fuji area) was used for travelling. Another travelling lantern, the *bura chōtin*, was roundish in the shape of a traditional tea-container and hung from a short stick.

There was another carrying lantern, the *yumihari chōtin*, named after its bow-shaped handle which was fitted parallel to the lantern. It was first used by warriors, but later taken over by the firemen. The flexible bamboo handle kept the lantern itself more stable when the owner moved about so that the candle was not put out so easily. These lanterns are still made. One other type of carrying lantern has remained popular, the *hōzuki chōtin* or 'ground-cherry lantern'. This small, round lantern has long been popular for carrying in lantern processions at festival time. They have always been painted red, or red and white, the colours of celebration, and many of them have been exported all over the world.

Fixed hanging lanterns were also made in various shapes and sizes. Lanterns similar to the one described in the craft section of this chapter have long been popular for advertising various kinds of establishment. This is the *takahari chōtin* (literally, 'stretched-tall lantern'), which is extended alongside the top of a bamboo pole, the top and bottom of the lantern stretched and tied to two bamboo crosspieces. These lanterns used to be put up in front of temples, official buildings, shops, teahouses and restaurants, and also carried at the head of funeral processions. Some of these uses continue today.

Such lanterns are normally decorated with the *mon* or insignia of a firm or family, and painted with suitable inscriptions in Chinese characters. *Kanji* is superbly decorative, quite apart from its meaning, and this tradition continues in the dazzling and spectacular neon signs where *kanji* dances in the night sky over the cities of modern Japan.

Two types of globe-shaped lantern, *tsuri chōtin*, are popular for lighting important parts of temples or shrines, often hung in double or triple rows, or as special lighting for festivals. Similar lanterns are also hung under the eaves of people's houses. Originally these were only hung out for the August festival of *o-bon*, when the souls of one's ancestors return home, but because of their beauty they are now hung out on any summer evening to create an atmosphere of peace and coolness to counteract the summer heat. Some old houses, just inside the door, still have a wooden rack fitted with four or five square paper lanterns, again decorated with the family *mon*, the whole rack of lanterns being placed outside the house for special family occasions and celebrations.

Above all else, the Japanese lantern is the symbol of celebration and festival, as evocative to the Japanese as the candles and lights of Christmas are to the Westerner. There are a multitude of festivals in Japan, some small, local affairs, others which take over a town for several days and have become national occasions. Each festival has its own atmosphere, just as it has its own meaning, but at many of them, in street or shrine, the climax comes at dusk with the lighting of the lanterns. They symbolize the spirit of celebration.

At no festival are the lanterns more spectacular than at the great Kyoto Gion Matsuri. This summer festival started in AD 869 as a procession from the Shinto Yasaka Shrine to ward off a plague. Today, each small district in the centre of Kyoto has its own float, a few as much as 24 m (26 yds) high. For a few nights before the great procession, the floats are displayed, and at

Bamboo Flutes

Plate 26 Zenmura-san sits in his workshop, considering which *shakuhachi* to work on next
Plate 27 A selection of repaired *shakuhachi*. (See Chapter Twelve)

each end a cascade of some forty lanterns rises like a glowing wall above the narrow, crowded streets. The Gion Matsuri gives Kyoto a unique character for those few nights, reminiscent in a way of the sacred and profane air of Seville during Holy Week.

Indeed, in Japan it is hard to draw any line between sacred and profane. Most of the famous festivals are based on Shinto shrines, partly because Buddhist celebrations are less public occasions. In Kyoto, religious and cultural capital, there are an average of five to six Shinto festivals each month. Many date back to the eighth or ninth centuries and the variety is great. Some Shinto festivals centre on an historical procession, some on traditional dancing, some on ritual drama, others on amateur sumo wrestling, and most of them display lanterns, often including charming small lanterns painted by local children. How far these festivals are religious is hard to judge. To most Japanese, one feels, they are simply part of the pattern of life and, without them, life would lose some of its meaning.

Making a Paper Lantern

Mitsugu Hiraide-san's geniality and energy permeated his large and busy workshop in Gifu, the major centre of this craft. The one enormous L-shaped room was full of women workers, some making paper lanterns, others finishing and packing, walled in on all sides by snaking piles of finished and half-finished folding lanterns of many different shapes and sizes. It was an ideal place to study this craft, illuminated by the patient explanation of Hiraide-san. But basically all paper lanterns are made in the same way and the process described here can be adapted to the different designs.

Making a Japanese paper lantern is an ingenious but simple process. The ingenuity is in the collapsible wooden frame around which the lantern is constructed, and which can easily be removed from inside the finished lantern. This frame consists of eight wooden wings, in the shape of the particular lantern, which are locked into position, top and bottom, with two wooden discs cut with eight radiating slots which receive the thinner top and bottom ends of the wings. After the frame has been assembled, thick rubber bands are put around the two necks of the frame. Each type of lantern requires a different frame.

After the frame has been assembled, it is mounted vertically in a simple revolving vice. Then bamboo cane bound with paper, fed from a large spool, is wound around the wooden frame, creating the skeleton of the lantern. The outer edge of each of the wings of the wooden frame is cut with small grooves which hold the spiralling bamboo cane in the correct position to allow the skeleton to concertina. When the skeleton is complete, light

76 The eight wings of the collapsible wooden frame are fitted into the slots of the top disc

77 The cane is wound in a continuing spiral around the wooden frame to form the skeleton

76

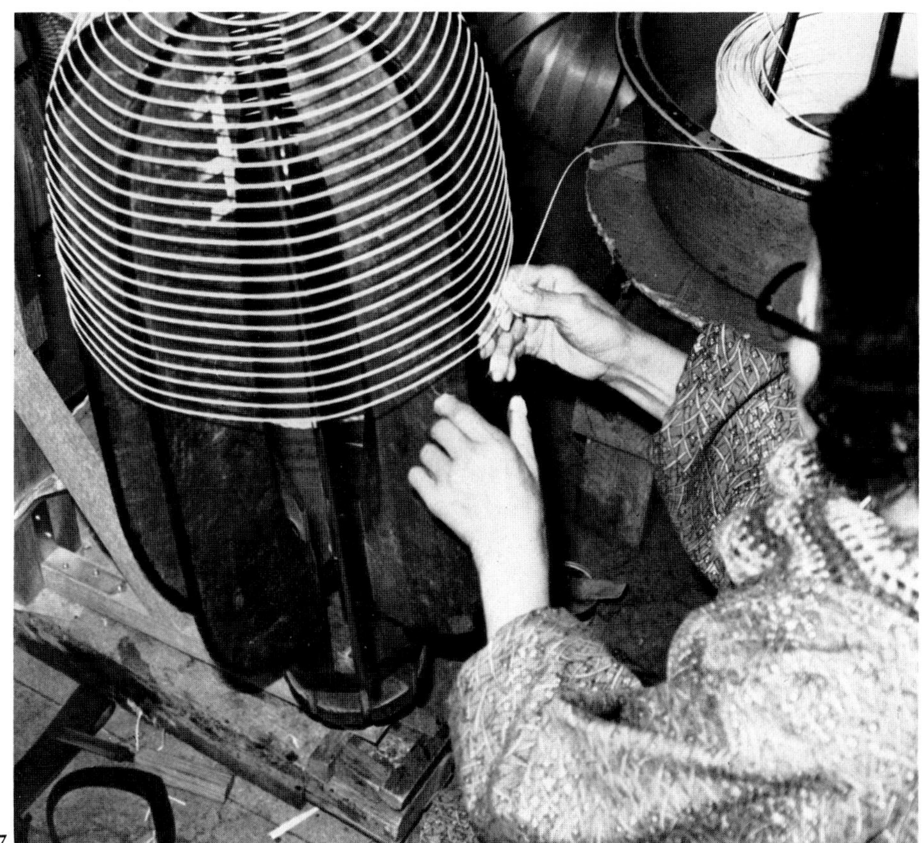

77

Sweetmeats

Plates 28 and 29 A boxed selection of dry sweetmeats, with seasonal shapes of flowers and leaves

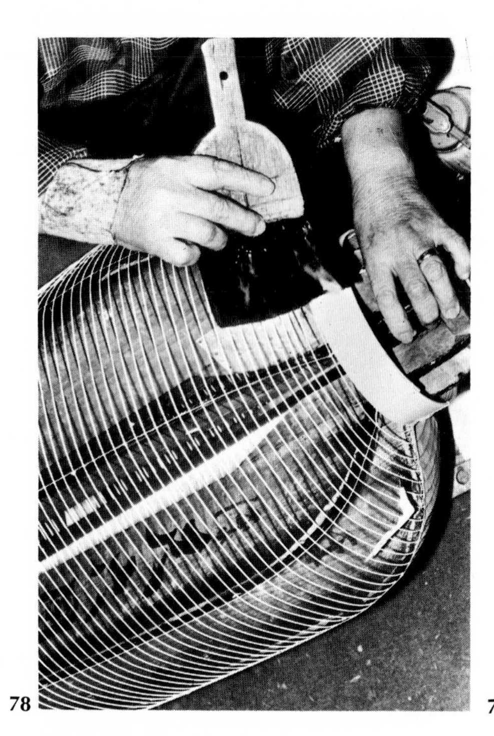

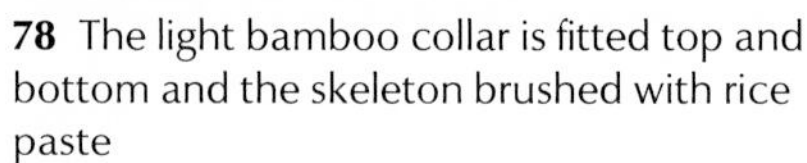

78 The light bamboo collar is fitted top and bottom and the skeleton brushed with rice paste

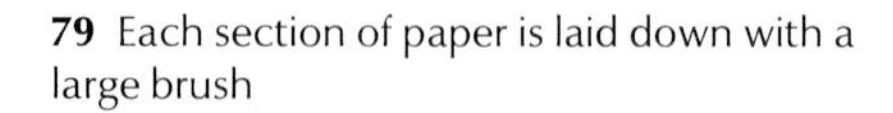

79 Each section of paper is laid down with a large brush

collars of bent bamboo are fixed to it, top and bottom, which later will be held firmly in position by an overlap of the papering.

A special locally-made paper is used for lanterns, thin enough to allow the skeleton to concertina, but sturdy enough to stand up to general use. Many of the light, highly fibrous Japanese papers are extremely strong, some as tough as fabric. It is, for example, almost impossible to tear a high-quality piece of handmade paper. The paper is glued to the skeleton in seven sections. First, the cane is brushed with rice paste, and the section of paper is laid down on the skeleton with a large brush. To lay these lengths of paper with accuracy and speed requires great skill. While the lantern is being papered it is held in a revolving vertical vice.

When the papering is complete, it is time to remove the collapsible frame, for after the rice-paste is dry the lantern will be stable. To do this, the wooden discs at either end are taken off, and carefully the eight wooden wings are turned together inside the lantern until they form a compact bundle that can be drawn out through the top of the lantern. With no other support the lantern now stands open on the floor. A gentle pressure will cause the lantern to concertina.

Many of the lanterns made in this workshop were standard designs; some were special orders, including one huge globular lantern about 1·5 m (c. 5 ft) high. The decoration varies and is done in different places. The Gifu workshop decorates some of its own lanterns and sends others away for finishing and decorating. For example, a well-known lantern and umbrella

80 Once the papering is complete, the wooden frame is dismantled inside the lantern and lifted out

shop in Kyoto buy 'blanks' which are decorated and fitted with collars at the back of the shop.

Basically, lantern decoration is either stencilled and painted, or painted freehand. Chinese characters (*kanji*) are the commonest form of decoration, whether the lanterns are for use in temples and shrines, or as signs or advertisements for shops, restaurants and other commercial premises. In many cases the characters are accompanied by a *mon*. The majority of lanterns are white, the Chinese characters painted in black. But coloured lanterns are also popular, particularly red lanterns with the decoration painted in reserved white panels. Nothing is prettier than the small red lanterns, each panel painted with a small white bird, that line the main street of Pontocho, one of the two geisha quarters of Kyoto. A few lanterns are more elaborately painted with floral patterns. There is a special Gifu lantern, mounted on a lacquered wooden stand, where the delicate lantern is painted with pretty patterns of flowers. Equally, anyone can walk into a lantern shop and order a lantern to be painted with their family name, their *mon* or whatever they may wish.

The lantern is finished by the addition of lacquered or black-painted collars top and bottom, fixed to the plain collars already mentioned. A black baseboard is fitted in the bottom collar and in the centre of this board is a small ring by which the bottom of the lantern can be secured if necessary. The top collar is fitted with a light wire handle, which can be used for hanging or carrying.

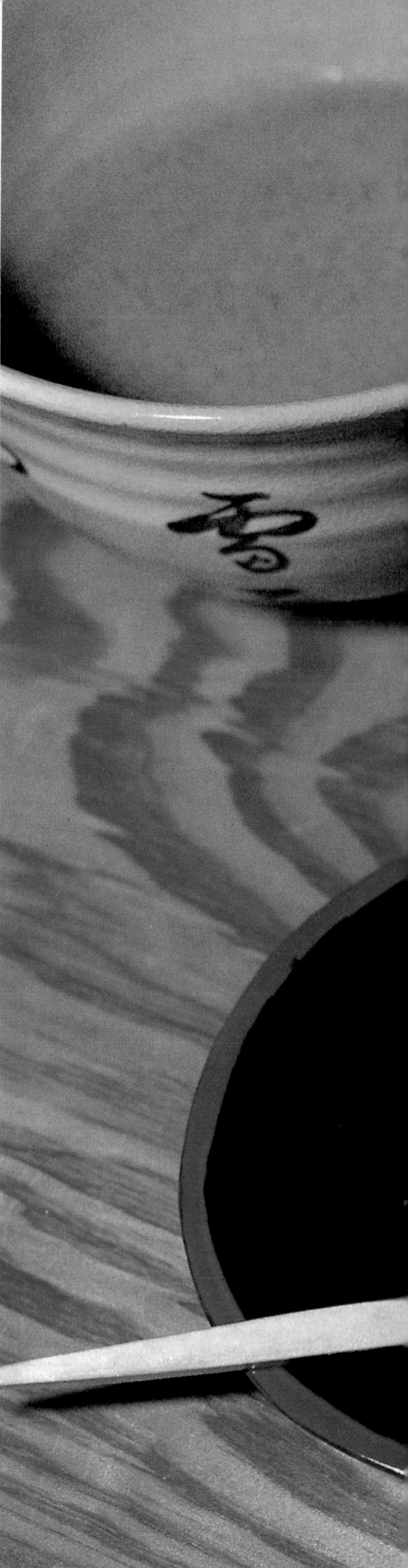

Raw Fish
Plate 30 A selection of high-quality *o-sushi* prepared by Futaya-san
Plate 32 Cheaper forms of *o-sushi* ready-packed in lunch boxes

Sweetmeats
Plate 31 A 'wet' sweetmeat on a lacquer dish with a wooden pick for eating. (See Chapter Thirteen)

81

81 The inside of the finished lantern

Practical Note

The problem here is obtaining the correct materials. The wooden frame is not difficult to make and adapt to different lantern shapes though it might be wise to make a prototype in cardboard. Anyone seriously considering making a paper lantern would be wise to start by consulting Sukey Hughes' admirable *'Washi', The World of Japanese Paper* (see Bibliography), which gives full details of the special papers used for lanterns and other Japanese crafts. This book is now easily obtainable. A wide variety of Japanese papers is now being sold around the world and special papers can sometimes be ordered.

The cane covered with paper will not be available anywhere and must be made. Long lengths of cane are easily bought and should be thinly bound with strips of a slightly absorbent paper. The purpose of the paper is to provide a key for the glue. Many Japanese craftsmen are moving to modern adhesives, so rice paste is unnecessary. For less-experienced craftsmen, and children, rigid lanterns are far easier to make and are still most attractive.

82 The lantern is painted freehand with Chinese characters. The lower side has a stencilled *mon* ready to be painted

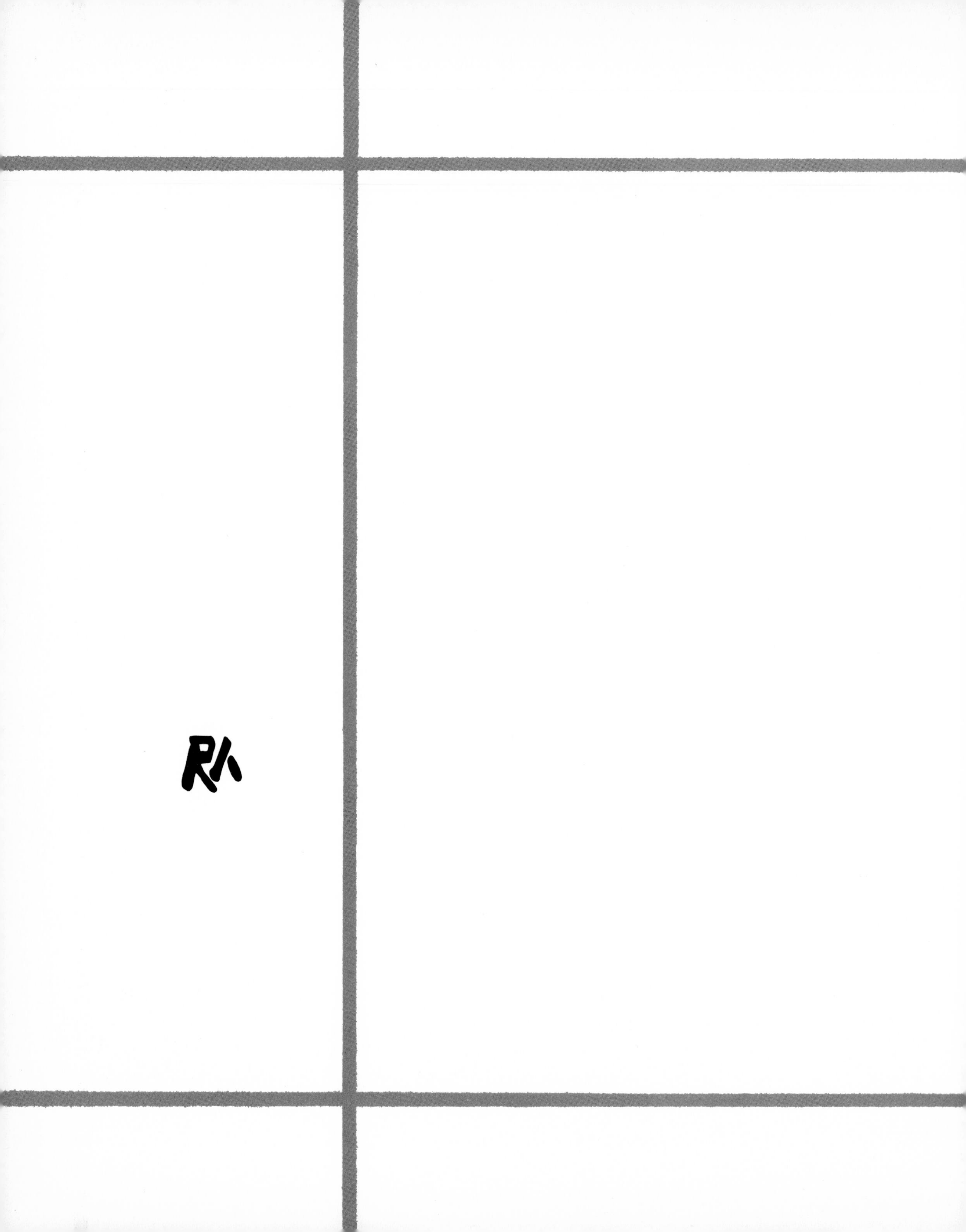

Music

12

Bamboo Flutes
Shakuhachi

The slightly melancholy sound of the *shakuhachi* evokes a mood of traditional Japan. Its music has a touch of sadness which echoes Japanese feelings about the transitoriness of human life. This end-blown bamboo flute, although so simple, is capable of an extraordinary musical range, particularly outside the restricted classical repertoire. The sound of the player's breath, far from being concealed, adds an enormous dimension to the music. The famous Zen priest, Watazumido, master of this technique, can draw a raging storm from this short length of bamboo. In a different direction, a few foreign players, notably the American, John Kaizan Neptune, have increased the range in jazz and swing music, where at times the *shakuhachi* takes on the sophistication of the clarinet. It is an extremely difficult instrument to play well and it is characteristic of the Japanese to have fashioned an instrument so musically fascinating from a short length of bamboo.

The *shakuhachi* came to Japan from China, via Korea, possibly as early as the late sixth century AD, when it was added to the small orchestra for *gagaku* court music and dancing. The orchestra already included two other types of flute, *fue* and *hichiriki*. This early *shakuhachi* had six finger-holes, was longer and thinner than the modern flute, and was made of bamboo, ivory or *shiritama* wood. Eight of these early flutes are preserved at Nara in the Shōsōin.

The flute's name comes from its Chinese measurement: *isshaku* (one *shaku*), *hassun* (eight *sun*). In modern terms that is 1·8 *shaku* or approximately 60 cm (c. 2 ft). This early flute, *kodai shakuhachi*, was played with other kinds of flutes, harp and drums in the court orchestra and it remained popular during most of the Heian period. But eventually it was dropped as it did not fit musically with the other instruments in the orchestra, and since then it has mainly been played as a solo instrument or to accompany songs.

The origins and development of the five-finger-hole *shakuhachi*, the standard flute of today, are uncertain, but there are a number of different theories. It is said that a priest, Hōtō-Kokushi, introduced it to Japan in the thirteenth century. The *hitoyogiri*, an end-blown, five-hole, shorter and thinner flute certainly did appear in Japan in the Muromachi period, said to have been played by wandering beggar-priests from China or South-East Asia. Later, in the Edo period, when the modern *shakuhachi* was finally developed, it was mainly used by the *Fuke* sect of Buddhism, whose wandering Zen priests, called *komusō*, wore deep baskets over their heads to symbolize their detachment from life, and played *shakuhachi* to beg for alms.

Such a hooded mendicant is shown in the charming *ukiyoe* print, 'Water Mirror', by Harunobu, in which a pretty girl, obviously suspecting that a handsome face is concealed by the basket, manages to catch a glimpse of the hidden face when it is reflected in a bowl of water she has placed on the ground. In real life the *komusō* seem to have played a rather more sinister role. One group, forging a licence from the first Shogun and other papers claiming early links with China, persuaded the Tokugawa government to give them official recognition and protection. In return these *komusō* agreed to join the Tokugawa's elaborate network of informers which helped the Shogunate defeat its opponents and maintain its oppressive regime.

It has been suggested that the earlier *hitoyogiri* was enlarged to the size of the heavier *shakuhachi* so that it could be used as a club. The *komusō* are said to have used their *shakuhachi* as weapons. Whatever the truth of this, undoubtedly the *Fuke* sect regarded playing the *shakuhachi* as its primary Zen discipline; a sacred instrument 'to blow Zen'. Although the *Fuke* sect and its temples were dissolved during the Meiji period, the great Kyoto Zen temple of Tofuku-ji has one small sub-temple devoted to the playing of *shakuhachi*. Here, each autumn, there is a *shakuhachi* festival where all players are welcome and the sound of the *shakuhachi* continuously fills the air from dawn till dusk.

Under Tokugawa regulations the *komusō*, outside their temples, could only teach samurai to play, but in the later Edo period the *shakuhachi* began to be played in the geisha quarters, and as an accompaniment for folk songs in the country. With the coming of the Meiji period in 1868 and the beginning of Westernization in Japan, the *Fuke* sect lost its privileges and was banned. But at the same time *shakuhachi*-playing spread among the general public. It was played with other traditional instruments such as *koto* (Japanese harp) and *samisen* (a stringed instrument which has no Western equivalent). New schools for teaching *shakuhachi* were founded and new music composed.

The two main schools controlling the teaching and playing of *shakuhachi* today are Kinko and Tozan. There are also other smaller schools together with a special style for playing folk music. The Kinko School was founded by Kurosawa Kinko (1710–71) in what was then Edo, now Tokyo. This school has its own system of notation, and a repertoire of some thirty-six solo pieces, based on *Fuke* music. Its *shakuhachi* also has a slightly different mouthpiece suited to this school's style of playing.

Nakao Tozan founded his school in the Osaka area in 1896. He composed his own music and in general this school has been more open-minded in accepting new music for the *shakuhachi*. The Tozan School's headquarters is in Kyoto but it is the practice of the school for its teachers to give lessons in their own homes. Their system of teaching is largely based on the student watching and listening to the master since the particular style of the school cannot be put down in notation. Somehow there remains a Zen quality in

83 Two lengths of *madake* bamboo; the left-hand one with root trimmed, the right-hand one with root complete

playing the *shakuhachi*. The music seems to come not only from correct fingering and breath control, but also from correct posture and state of mind.

Japanese custom and tradition have imposed severe limits on Japanese music and it is not only the *shakuhachi* that is finding a new range under foreign influences which lead to more flexible attitudes and make room for experiment. Perhaps these traditional attitudes to their music throw some light on a question that is so frequently asked today: 'Are the Japanese creative, or merely brilliant copyists?' For centuries music has played an important part in Japanese culture yet, by world standards, Japan has produced no great music. Mostly Japanese music has been the servant of other arts, an accompaniment to dance, drama, recitation and songs. It has served these purposes perfectly but has not been allowed to expand outside the rigid limits that social needs and tradition have laid down for it. The same seems true of so much in Japanese life and such conditions inhibit the creative spirit, whether it be in music or scientific experiment. The genius of the Japanese in design, in the exploitation of ideas and materials and an incredible refinement of taste, all strongly suggest that for centuries their natural creativity has been frustrated and limited by the nature of Japanese society. 'Everything in its place, and a place for everything' could certainly describe Japan from the beginning of the Edo period, and to some extent before that. Tradition is double-edged. While it protects, it may also destroy; while supporting the growing plant, eventually it may also strangle it.

Making a Bamboo Flute

Kazan Zenmura-san has been making *shakuhachi* for sixteen years. As a young man he learned to play the *shakuhachi* but, finding he could not afford a good flute, he tried to make one. He became so interested that he studied with a master-craftsman for five years and since then has worked on his own. He has established a high reputation among both Japanese and foreign players.

Zenmura-san works in his small modern house in the northern outskirts of Kyoto where the housing development is overtaking the remaining rice fields. His house is easy to identify. Lengths of bamboo are stacked around the front yard. Through the front door one can see the main room, a crowded yet well-ordered workshop, with rows of saws, files and other tools racked on the walls; the floor cluttered with heavy screw-clamps, low box-benches and drying-boxes. All around are *shakuhachi*, most in various stages of manufacture, some returned by players for repair. Seated on the floor, a striking pink vest buttoned up to his neck, Zenmura-san

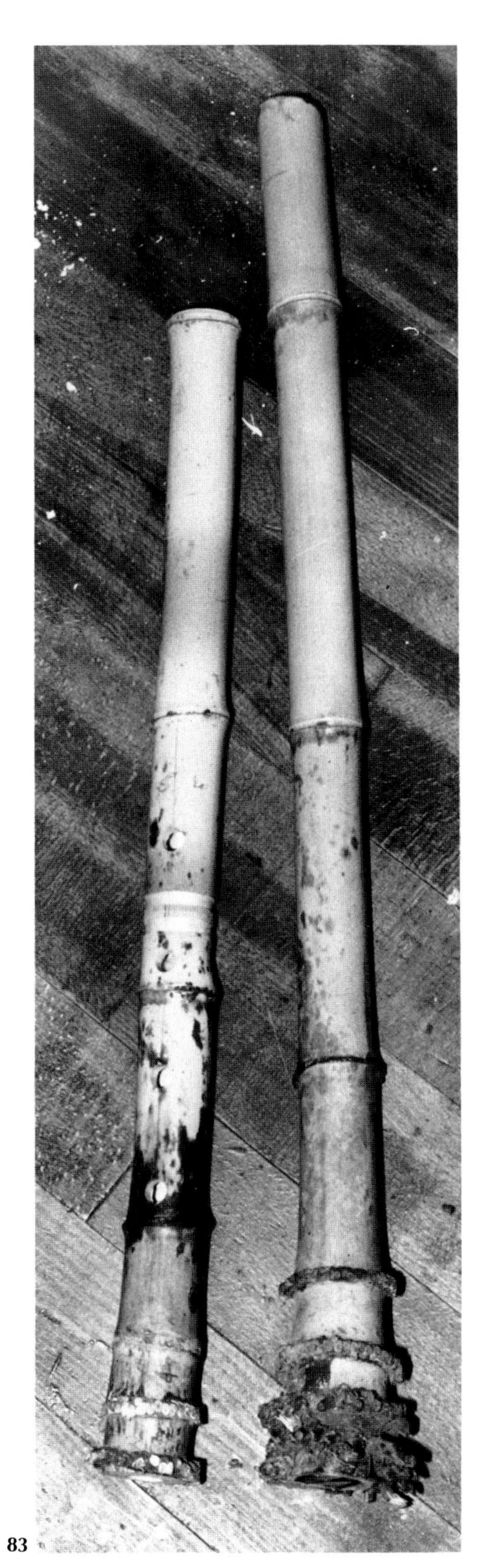
83

enthusiastically explains his craft. A large oil stove makes the room stifling and, while his wife picks her way across the cluttered floor to serve tea, Zenmura-san begins to demonstrate the making of a *shakuhachi*.

The *shakuhachi* is made from a straight-stemmed species of bamboo called *madake* (botanical name: *Phyllostachys bambusoides*), grown in the island of Shikoku. This thick-walled bamboo is less likely to split, and is the only bamboo of suitable size that polishes to a pleasant colour after it is dried. The bamboo is cut at root level, the root forming a knobbled bell-shaped end to the flute. The bamboo is cut between October and March, usually in lengths of about 55 cm (21·6 in), the average circumference being 10 to 11 cm (3·9–4·3 in.). The musical quality of the flute will largely depend on the right qualities in the bamboo: the hardness of the wood and the correct shape of the stem and root.

After the bamboo has been cut, the oils are removed from the stems by drying them in the winter sun for about two months; the summer sun would be too strong. During drying the bamboo changes colour from green to white. It is then soaked in an insecticide, and afterwards stored in a cool, dry place for two to three years.

A craftsman keeps a large stock of drying and dried stems, selecting a suitable stem when he is ready to make a new *shakuhachi*. Normally, Zenmura-san makes a number of instruments at the same time, although they will be at different stages of construction. It would not be economic to make one at a time. The standard modern *shakuhachi* is 54·5 cm (21·4 in.) long, though there are twelve recognized lengths ranging from 39·4 to 75·7 cm (15·5–29·8 in.). Occasionally, even longer ones are made, but these are something of a 'stunt'. The depth of note increases with the length. If the root is damaged, it is trimmed and filed smooth as necessary, but preferably the root is only cleaned and left in its knobbly form, giving the *shakuhachi* its unique and rather strange appearance.

Often the natural curve in the bamboo must be straightened. The stem is heated over a small Japanese brazier which burns oak charcoal. The bamboo is slightly scorched in this process, which gives the wood an attractive dark shading when the flute is finally polished. The colour can vary from a pale honey to very dark brown. The bamboo is then gently straightened in a special vice (*manriki*), kept under tension for about five minutes until the bamboo has cooled.

Nowadays, the next stage is to cut the stem in two, the upper half about 5 cm (2 in.) longer than the lower section. This makes it easier to work on the inside, and can help in placing the finger-holes correctly. Next, at the upper end of the lower half the inside is cleaned out enough to allow a bamboo ring to be inserted. This forms the joint between the two sections of the flute. The ring is 6 to 7 cm (2·4–2·7 in.) long and is made by another craftsman.

84 The length of bamboo is cut in two, and a ring of bamboo (shown here in the middle) is inserted. On the left, the ring is in position

84

85 The oblique angle is sawn on the front of the mouthpiece

Now the five finger-holes are bored, four on top and one below. The holes are placed in different positions according to the length of the *shakuhachi*. There are also *shakuhachi* with seven and nine holes. The standard flute, with five holes, produces the pitches D F G A C with all holes closed. The *shakuhachi* spans three octaves, though normally only two are used. Today the holes are made with a modern power-drill and afterwards shaped and finished with small chisels and files. The finished hole is slightly oval in shape and flairs to a greater width at the base. Some players alter the finger-holes of a new flute quite drastically to suit their own style of fingering, enlarging them or altering the position. This is a craft based on musicality and experience, not an exact science, so it is impossible to give exact instructions about the position of the finger-holes. In older flutes the tuning will not always correspond to Western pitches. Judging by the *shakuhachi* in Zenmura-san's workshop, their lifespan for playing is about forty years.

Now come the two processes which test the main skills of the *shakuhachi*-maker. These are the making of the mouthpiece, and the tuning of the flute by lining the inside with plaster. While working, the craftsman, who is seated on the floor, rests the *shakuhachi* in the notches cut around the upper sides of a rectangular box. This provides him with a low 'bench'. With notches on all sides, the *shakuhachi* can be held steady at any angle according to the need of the process in hand.

To make the mouthpiece, a very slight angle is marked along the top of the *shakuhachi*, and a sharper, oblique angle is marked on the front of the flute. These two angles are then cut with a fine saw and this first shaping of the mouthpiece is smoothed with a file. Then the front, oblique angle must be given a concave curve which is marked with a wooden masterblock and exactly shaped.

A wafer-thin insert of ivory, water-buffalo horn or, more recently, black acrylic plastic, must now be sunk immediately behind the oblique blowing edge. Here Zenmura-san is using black plastic. It is this thin insert that splits the player's breath and produces the sound. The process is on such a 'wafer-thin' scale, it is hard to describe and to photograph. First, using fine chisels, a narrow slit is cut behind the oblique angle to house the black plastic insert. Zenmura-san works with a strip of black plastic for ease of handling, and fashions the insert at one end, shaping and tailoring it with files and sandpaper. The plastic insert must fit the slit perfectly. Next a very thin band of silver is fitted around the plastic insert. The silver and plastic insert is then placed in the slit and held secure with a few drops of ordinary bonding glue; 'as used for fishing', said Zenmura-san. The remaining length of plastic is then sawn off, and the mouthpiece is finished with further filing.

It sometimes happens that a certain mouthpiece will suit the mouth of a particular player. In various ways the *shakuhachi* is a particularly personal

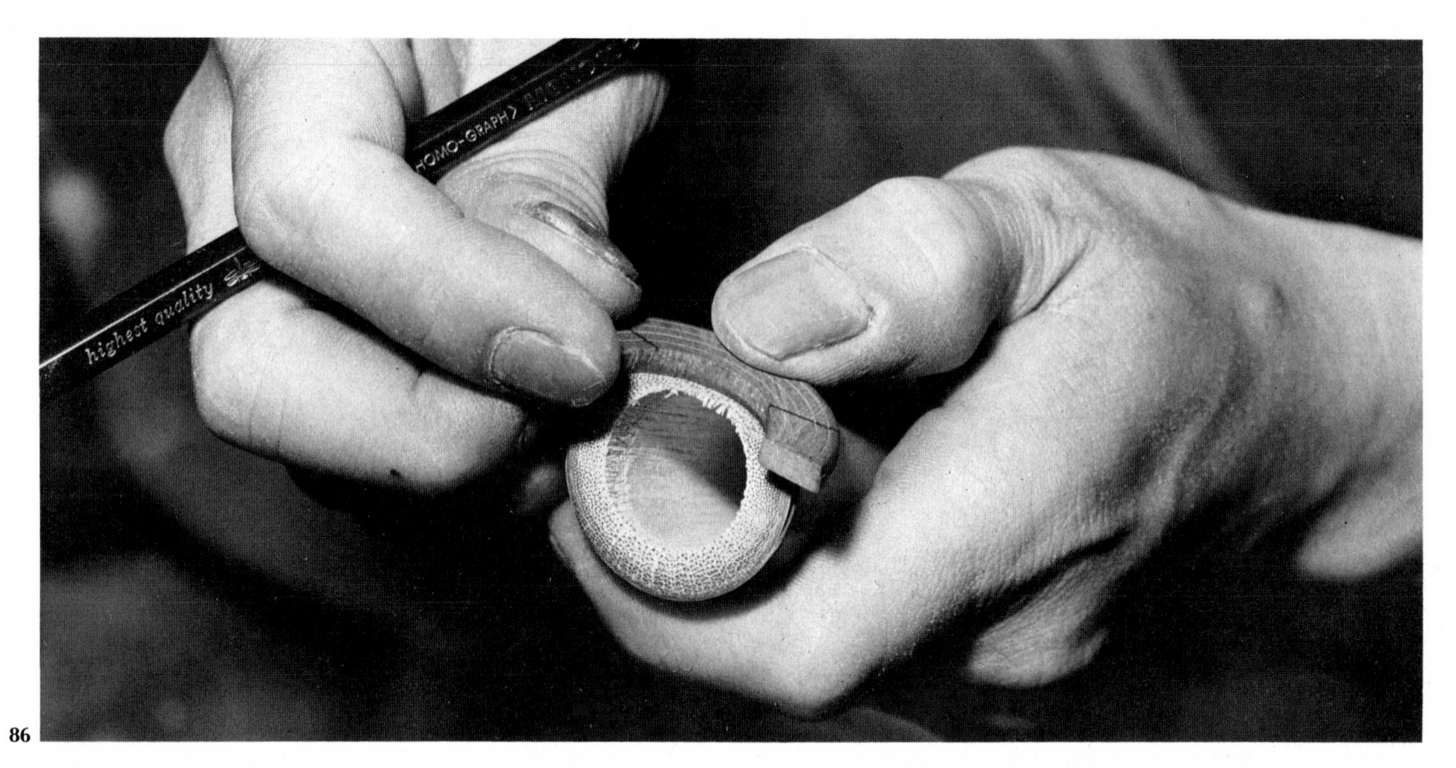

86

86 The concave curve of the front, oblique angle is marked with the masterblock

87 A fine slot is cut behind the oblique angle to house the acrylic insert

88 The first fitting of the acrylic insert into its slot

instrument, in which the qualities of a flute, each one unique, must be matched to the personal requirements of the player. In Zenmura-san's workshop there were at least fifty *shakuhachi*, some just made, others there for repair. Asked to choose the best flute in his workshop, not surprisingly he chose the one he plays himself.

The next stage is to clean and shape the inside of the *shakuhachi* in order to tune it. This requires not only manual skill but also considerable ability in playing the flute and an acute musical ear. Small-headed files and brushes on long handles are used to clear, smooth and clean the inside. Normally the diameter is made slightly smaller from the mouthpiece, 2·3 cm (0·9 in.), to the base, 1·8 cm (0·7 in.). To tune the flute, the interior is lined with a coating of plaster applied with a long-handled spatula. Zenmura-san uses two kinds of dental plaster, adjusting the tuning by the application of exactly the correct thickness.

When the tuning is correct and the plaster dry, the inside of the *shakuhachi* is painted with an undercoat of lacquer. The lacquered flutes are then put in a box to dry, the interior of which is kept slightly moist with pads of wet sponge. During the rainy season the flutes are dried for one day; at all other times for two to three days. Next, a fine, smooth finish is given to the inside of the *shakuhachi* with a clear, natural lacquer, coloured with either black or red mercury paste. This lacquer is applied with brushes made of women's hair. Best is the hair of women pearl-divers, as the sea salt makes

87

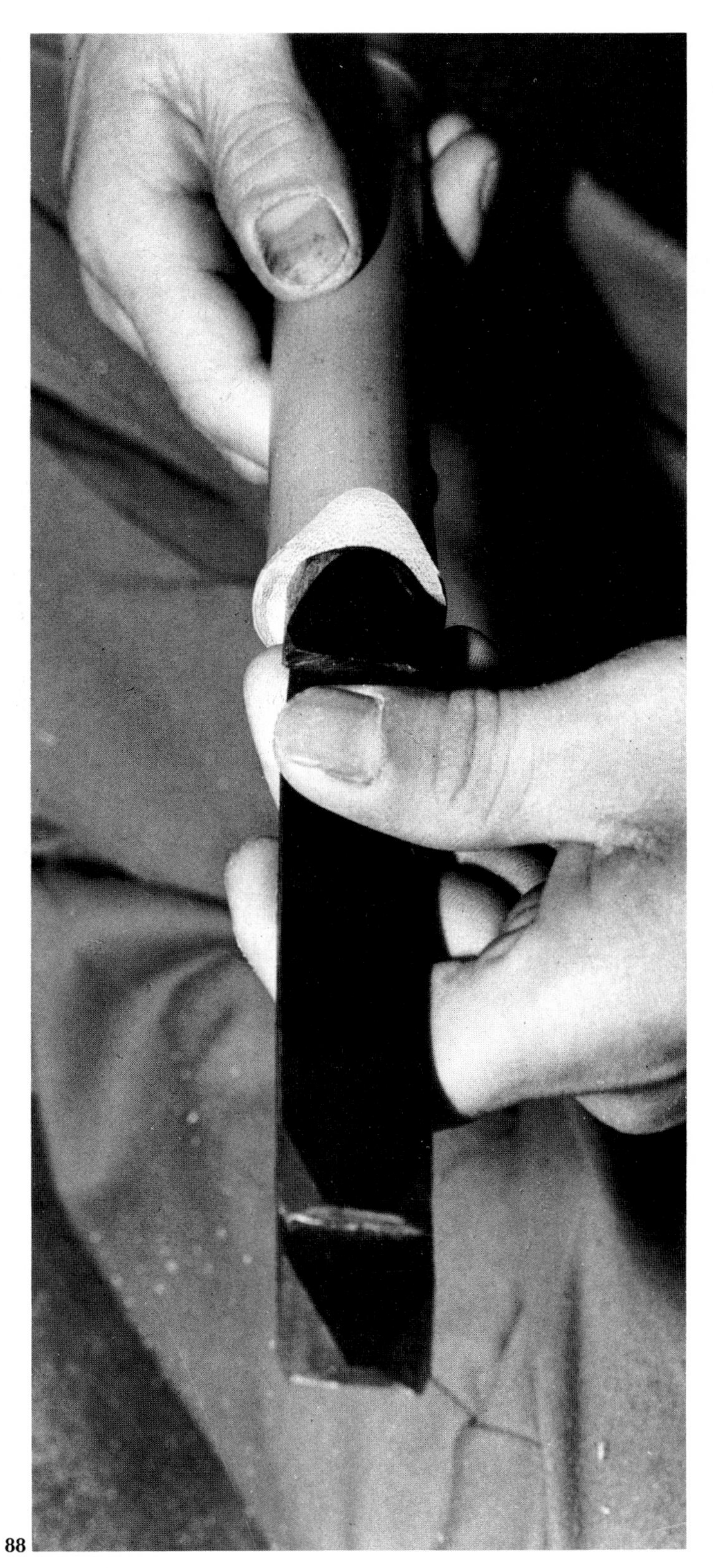
88

89 Three finished mouthpieces, showing the concave curve of the front oblique angle, and the thin line of silver between the acrylic and the bamboo

their hair particularly absorbent. The lacquer is also applied to the joint and the insides of the finger-holes with a smaller brush. The flutes are again dried in the moist box. Now the final finish is given to the *shakuhachi*. The joint is decoratively bound with gold or silver wire, and the bamboo is finely polished with a soft deer-skin leather.

Zenmura-san can make about ten *shakuhachi* each month, fitting in the different processes and the drying times. He also repairs about ten *shakuhachi* each month, binding the splits with nylon thread. However, if a *shakuhachi* warps, it is beyond repair. Zenmura-san is a member of the Tozan School and one of about twenty makers belonging to it.

Good bamboo *shakuhachi* have become extremely expensive. Today a good flute might well cost 175,000 yen or more; a very good one far more! In recent times *shakuhachi* have been made of maple wood and moulded plastic, and these cheap instruments are adequate for beginners. But as a player develops, if he makes good progress, he will continually feel the need for better flutes. A keen player will almost certainly own several *shakuhachi*, to match both music and mood, each one different in such qualities as volume, tone and musical colour. Part of the pleasure of playing this fascinating instrument is the continual search for the 'ideal' *shakuhachi*. That is why players often follow the example of Kazan Zenmura and become makers.

Practical Note

If the intricacy of the above description leaves the reader somewhat dismayed, let me offer something of an antidote. I went to discuss the first draft of this chapter with Clif Karhu, who not only makes seals (see Chapter Nine), prints, and paints brilliantly, but is also a good maker of *shakuhachi*. As I was blinding him with the science of acrylic inserts and dental plaster, he picked up a beautiful-looking *shakuhachi* and played some extremely mellow scales. 'Zenmura-san?' I asked. 'No,' replied Clif, 'I made it last night. Just used a bamboo insert. Cleaned out the inside with a dental drill and left it alone.' With a wry smile he played another extremely mellow scale.

So I offer only two pieces of advice to those who wish to make a *shakuhachi*. If you are not musical, don't! If you are, use the detailed description in this chapter as a basis for experiment. It is really a very simple instrument. Your first flute may be a failure but you will get there if you persist, and your hundredth *shakuhachi* may be a masterpiece. *Gambatte* (hang in there)!

お茶菓子

お鮨

Food

13

Sweetmeats *O-Kashi*

Many Japanese words are difficult to translate because they contain a concept which does not relate to Western culture. *O-kashi* is such a word, for which I have chosen the old-fashioned word, sweetmeat, as this hovers between the more modern words, cake, and candy or sweets, whose Western connotations do not convey the special nature of *o-kashi*. It is true, and confusing, that some *o-kashi* resemble cakes, while others look like candies, but the Japanese do not see either kind as a cake or a candy. *O-kashi* exist in their own right, mainly belonging to the formal world of the tea ceremony or, at least, to formal domestic occasions when *o-kashi* are served with the thick, whipped tea of the tea ceremony. A short history of Japanese confectionery may help to put *o-kashi* in their correct place.

In the past, the Japanese ate two meals a day, and puddings and sweets have never been a feature of their cuisine. Formally, fresh or dried fruit was eaten between meals, and today fresh fruit is sometimes served at the end of a meal. The word *kashi* in fact derives from the word for fruit. During the Nara period some Chinese sweets were introduced to Japan and, although made of grain or soya beans, they were called Chinese fruit. Sugar also came to Japan at this time. It was made by boiling sugar cane and was black in colour. For several centuries it was used by the aristocracy as a remedy for chest complaints and did not really come into general use in Japanese cooking and confectionery until the Meiji period.

From the Heian period various sweet confections were offered on special occasions at both Shinto shrines and Buddhist temples, and these later became confectionery for the aristocracy, though down the centuries special cakes and the like became associated with and were sold in the precincts of many shrines and temples. Similarly, certain types of cakes became associated with certain towns, and these confections still provide the perfect souvenir for the Japanese tourist to take back to family and friends.

With the development of the essentially aristocratic tea ceremony in the fifteenth century, certain types of these early sweetmeats came to be served as part of the meal accompanying the ceremony or on their own. They became an integral part of the tea ceremony and both they and the ritual surrounding their serving were elaborated. It was here that *o-kashi* branched off from the general development of Japanese confectionery, taking on a special and ceremonial nature. General confectionery was influenced in the sixteenth century with the coming of the Portuguese and other Europeans, when such things as sponge cake were introduced. The taste for Western cakes developed considerably during the Meiji period when chocolate was finally introduced, and exploded into a vast industry after the Second World War when the incipient Japanese 'sweet tooth' came into its own after centuries of frustration!

Today, if you love cakes, forget Paris, forget Vienna, and take the first plane for Tokyo. Japan is the land of cakes in every shape, sort and size, from the exquisitely modelled *o-kashi* for the tea ceremony to the almost equally exquisite imitations of French gateaux and Viennese torte. But in Japan cakes are not merely food; they are an integral part of Japanese life. By a strange coincidence, just as I started to write this page, the bell of my Kyoto apartment rang. It was my landlady distributing 'apology presents' to each tenant on behalf of our neighbours opposite who are just about to demolish and rebuild their house. The present is an obligatory token of regret for the inconvenience they will be causing everyone in the immediate neighbourhood. As there is potential friction in this situation, they do not deliver the 'apology' themselves but, in a typical Japanese way, use a neutral middleman who can absorb any expressions of indignation without harming longterm neighbourly relations. The present, typically enough, was a beautifully wrapped box of cakes presented in a traditional and seasonal style. The wrapping paper was patterned with swirling autumn leaves and the moulded cakes represented the pairs of pine needles that fall in autumn. Everything was elegantly Japanese, yet strangely the actual cake mixture was a delicious crisp sponge.

A small present must be given on many occasions in Japan and cakes, in their various forms, are one of the currencies of daily life. Famous cake shops receive pilgrims almost like a well-known shrine or temple might. Kyoto has long been famous for its traditional cakes and must boast several hundred cake shops whose trade depends so entirely on souvenirs and present-giving that the wrapping has become as important as the contents. The famous shops specializing in *o-kashi* have a particular aura. Equally amazing and equally numerous are the shops now selling French-style patisseries, mountainous confections of fruit and whipped cream. Apart from the cake shops, there are hundreds of coffee shops, with such suitable names as 'Elegant' or 'Café Mozart'.

The shops making and selling *o-kashi* have a traditional and more formal air, as befitting anything connected with the tea ceremony. These sweetmeats are the aristocrats of Japanese confectionery and extremely expensive. *O-kashi* are basically of two kinds, 'wet' (*omogashi*), and 'dry' (*higashi*). The wet variety are basically made of sweetened bean paste and bean jam and are usually served with thick green tea. The dry sweetmeats, which look more like candies, are kinds of rice biscuit or rice jelly, and are usually served with thin green tea, though on occasions the two types are served together.

O-kashi have been separated from the formal meal sometimes served at the tea ceremony. The sweetmeats are now served on their own when the guests first assemble for the tea ceremony. There is a complicated etiquette

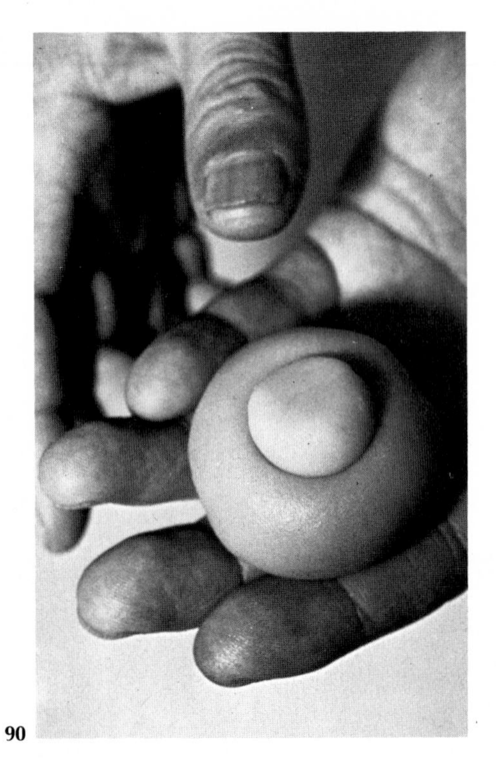

90

90 The smaller white ball is pressed into the indentation made in the pink ball of dough

for serving, accepting and eating *o-kashi,* which differs somewhat with the serving of *omogashi* and *higashi.* For the larger wet sweetmeats a tiny wooden pick is provided to cut the *omogashi* into manageable mouthfuls. For the beginner, the correct and elegant manipulation of *o-kashi,* dishes, wooden pick and paper napkin, is far more problematical than handling the knife and fork of the Western world.

O-kashi are extremely beautiful, particularly when set out for serving at the tea ceremony in a handsome pottery sweetmeat bowl, or carefully 'scattered' like bright flowers across a lacquer dish. The design of both wet and dry is always seasonal – flowers for each month, autumn leaves, a crane or Japanese nightingale. Each famous *o-kashi* shop has its specialities, its own recipes and its individual style in modelling its sweetmeats.

We were lucky to be allowed behind the scenes of the famous Kyoto shop, Tawaraya, an *o-kashi* shop that dates back to the eighteenth century. In 1775 it received its present name when it was taken over by one of its own workers, Sobei Tawara. It was originally situated by the Imperial Palace, but during the struggles of 1862 the owner was killed and the shop destroyed. It was re-started in 1924, a little further north, by Tomejiro Ishihara-san, still alive at eighty-two. The shop is now run by his son, Yoshimasa Ishihara-san. Their *o-kashi* are famous all over Japan and sold by many other shops apart from their own two shops in Kyoto. The artistry with which their sweetmeats are made is remarkable, and it epitomizes the skill and care that is put into Japanese food to give it a beautiful and attractive appearance. This, certainly in the case of *o-kashi,* is far more important than the taste.

Making Sweetmeats

The high-quality traditional sweetmeats served at the tea ceremony described here are made from various kinds of bean, prepared to make a kind of paste or dough, which is then stuffed with a bean jam made from a different kind of bean. There are two kinds of bean paste for this type of sweetmeat, *neriki* and *konashi.* There is not much difference between them though it is said that *konashi* is easier to work and shape. The bean paste used in this description is *konashi.* Both types of paste or dough are made by a laborious process of soaking and boiling haricot beans. Then the 'cream' is sieved off and mixed carefully with a paste of rice flour and water, and slightly sweetened with sugar. The resultant dough is then thoroughly kneaded. For the cake described here some wheat flour was also added, and after kneading the dough was then steamed. Finally, some malt honey was added to the dough to make it softer and more pliable for modelling.

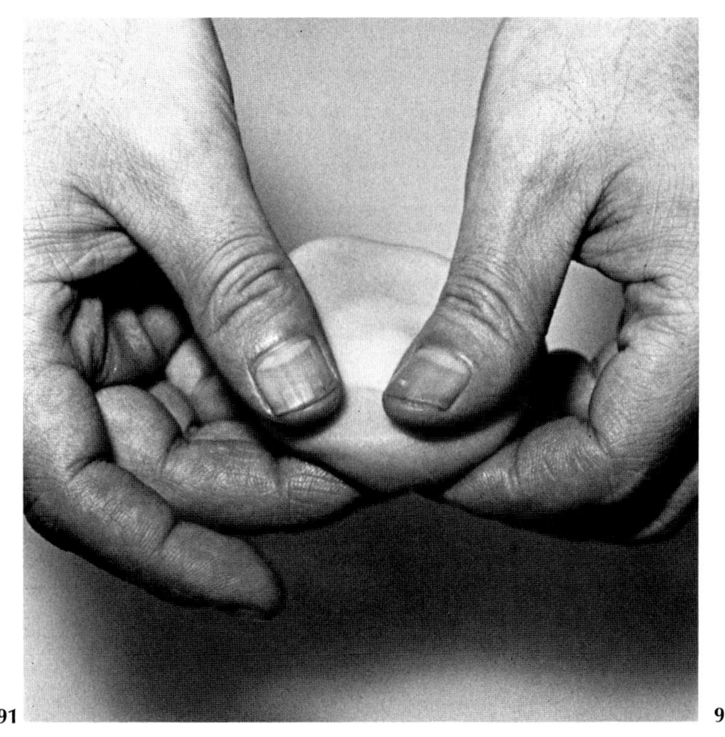

91

92

91 The two balls are compressed to form a flattened disc

92 A ball of bean jam is placed on the pink disc which is then wrapped around it

The cake we saw being made was a budding paeony flower (for July) of soft pink and white with yellow stamens. The processes may appear extremely simple, but in fact the modelling of these sweetmeats requires considerable artistry since, in their ephemeral way, they achieve the beauty of miniature sculpture. The appeal to the eye is greater than that to the palate as, certainly to the Westerner, the sweetmeats are rather solid in texture and bland in flavour.

First, the white dough is divided and some set aside. The remainder is dyed pink, using red plum for the dye. The dyes are always natural materials, such as egg yolk for yellow and green tea for green. Now both the white and pink dough are made into small balls, each pink ball about three times the size of the white balls. The cook then takes a pink ball and with his knuckle or finger makes a deep, circular indentation into which he presses a smaller white ball. Then, using the fingers of both hands, he flattens the pink ball, and the white ball contained in it, until the dough has become a flattened pink disc with a white centre.

At this point, the flattened disc is turned over, so that the white dough is now underneath. Then a ball of red bean jam is placed on the centre of the pink disc and wrapped in the dough which is re-formed into a ball. The bean jam is made from the *adzuki* bean mashed into a paste and boiled down with sugar. The bean jam is sweeter than the dough, but not as sweet as the average Western cake.

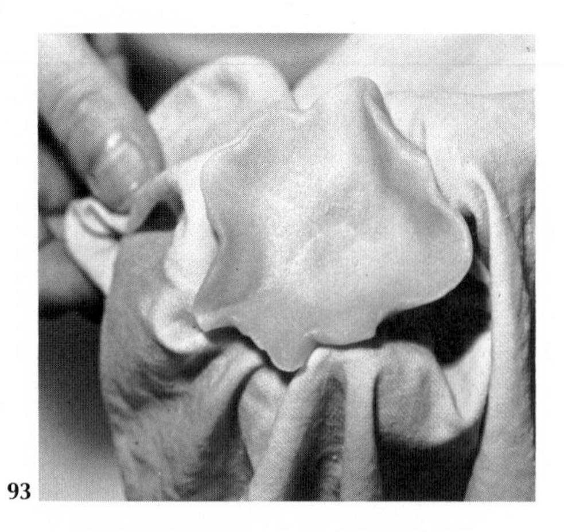

93 The white dough is pinched and spread and then placed in a damp cloth

94 Yellow-dyed dough is forced through a sieve to form the stamen threads

95 The stamens are applied to the finished bud

The next process is the trickiest, in which the ball of pink and white dough is given the delicate appearance and surface texture of budding paeony petals whose pink and white colouring softly blend and merge. First the ball of dough is turned so that the white base is uppermost. Then, extremely carefully, the white dough is pinched and spread to provide the delicate unfolding petal forms. Now the dough ball with its white 'flower head' is placed in a damp cloth which is squeezed tight to close the area around the tips of the petals. The action of squeezing the cloth also slightly blurs together the pink and white doughs and gives the whole peony bud a slightly pinched and textured surface, creating the illusion of a bud about to break open into full flower. The main body of the bud is pink and on the opening petals pink and white shade off into each other. This method of modelling with a damp cloth is used for several classic sweetmeat models.

Now a yellow-dyed dough is gently pushed through a sieve, and the threads that emerge are placed, using chopsticks, in the mouth of the opening bud to simulate the yellow stamens. The *o-kashi* is complete and will now be packed in a wrapping as elegant as itself. This is a wet sweetmeat, or *omogashi*, with a limited shelf-life, and since it remains soft, it must be handled with care up to the moment of serving.

Practical Note

Most of the ingredients, or satisfactory substitutes, for these sweetmeats are readily available, and recipes can be found in various books on Japanese cooking. Making the doughs and bean jams is laborious rather than particularly skilful. The charm and beauty of these sweetmeats lie in the seasonal choice of subject and the exquisite stylized modelling. As such, they could provide a fresh inspiration for cooks wishing to work with familiar Western materials such as marzipan or various kinds of icing. A number of books on the tea ceremony illustrate a variety of *o-kashi*, both wet and dry. The Japanese sweetmeat points the way to a whole area of experiment, both in materials and subject matter. As always, skill derives from practice.

94

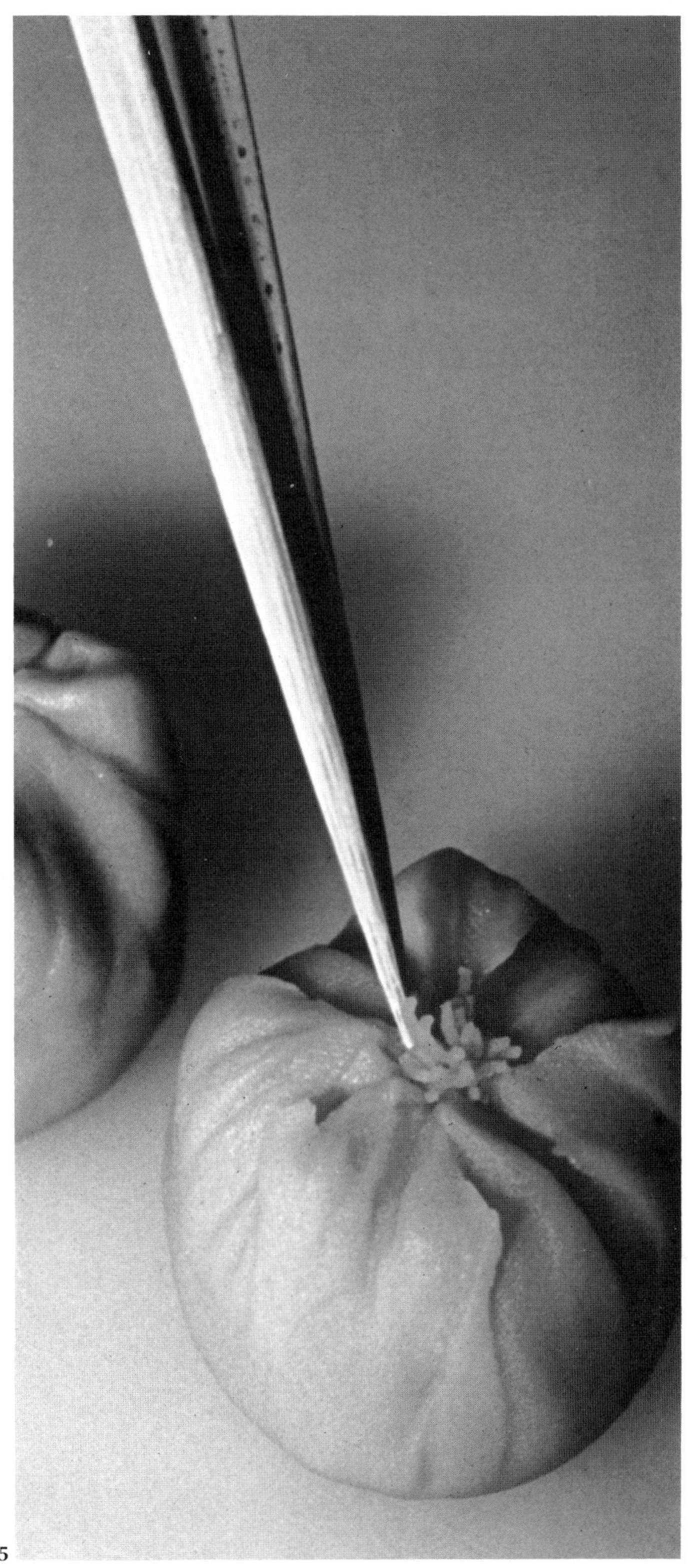

95

14

Raw Fish
O-Sushi

O-sushi is not so much a food as a way of life. If one is forced to name Japan's national dish, then it must be *o-sushi*. Raw fish is served in two ways in Japan: as *sashimi*, where slices of raw fish are served alone, often as the first dish of a Japanese meal; and as *o-sushi*, where basically slices of raw fish are served on long, flattened balls of a special vinegared and slightly sweetened rice in mouth-sized pieces, though there are other additions and variations in the enormous repertoire of *o-sushi*. The simpler forms of *o-sushi* are made at home, but usually it is eaten in a *sushi* bar or delivered to one's home from the bar in circular lacquer dishes. The *sushi* restaurant, which serves nothing else, is called a bar since the afficionados only sit up at the counter and the very small *sushi* shops have no tables. *O-sushi* is eaten in every possible way: it can be a full meal or just a good excuse for drinking. Celebrations, a nice day or simply a good mood call for *o-sushi* from mid-morning through to late in the evening. Anyone worthy of his *o-sushi* has his favourite *sushi* bar (all others are terrible) while the true enthusiasts not only eat *o-sushi* with their fingers but speak a special *sushi*-bar dialect and use a method of counting unique to *sushi*. *O-sushi* is, of course, eaten in all seasons. Only the ingredients change.

This was by far the most enjoyable research we undertook for this book and we were extremely lucky to be allowed to make it in Clif Karhu's favourite *sushi* bar, owned by one of the best *sushi* cooks in Kyoto, Yoshihisa Futaya-san. He took us early in the morning to visit the Kyoto fish market and later revived us with both his skill and his superb *o-sushi*. There is a slight neighbourhood joke concerning Futaya-san's shop that I am sure, because of his extreme good humour, he would not mind me telling. Since he always chooses the best-quality fish and since everything in his restaurant is of the highest quality, his prices are high. It so happens that next door is one of those student *sushi* bars where they slice their low-quality fish so thin, that in comparison they practically appear to be giving away their *o-sushi*. Over the years a large number of foreigners, through an understandable confusion, have suffered two very different kinds of *sushi*-shocks. Futaya-san must, on occasions, have seen some foreigners turn very pale when handed their bill!

The earliest origins of *sushi* seem to be associated with preserving various kinds of fish; a tenth-century book records that certain districts paid tribute to the Emperor with this kind of early *sushi*, though at that time the fish was not bedded on rice. It is said that rice was first added in the sixteenth century, to speed the pickling process, and that shortly people began to prefer a sweetened rice. At this time the two main kinds of *sushi* were *nare*, meaning 'tame', and *haya*, meaning 'quick'. With *nare* the fish took two months to season, with *haya* four weeks. From the Edo period *haya* became the popular form of *sushi*; vinegar was added to the rice, the fish pressed on to the beds of rice and this 'cake' cut into small pieces. *Haya zushi* was first mainly made in Kansai around Osaka; in the late seventeenth century it was introduced to Edo (Tokyo), and in the early eighteenth century the first *sushi* shops opened. A book of 1687 in fact mentions an existing Edo *sushi* shop which is considered the oldest in Japan.

After this the history becomes more complicated with the development of a number of different types of *sushi*, with considerable local variations. Of these, *nigiri-zushi*, with fish on balls of rice, became the most popular. Today *nigiri-zushi* is considered the Tokyo style, while *nare-zushi* is the basis of the Osaka style. However, the two styles can be mixed, and they are extended by various other forms of *o-sushi* – which use seaweed, vegetables, fried tofu and sweet omelette, besides the wide range of fish. Winter and spring are the best seasons for *o-sushi*. Futaya-san offers eighteen varieties of *o-sushi* in winter but only twelve during the summer. Some specialities, such as the delicious crabs' brains, are only available for a few weeks during the year.

The heart of every *sushi* bar is the long counter of spotless white cypress at which the serious seat themselves, ordering *o-sushi* piece by piece from the refrigerated glass cabinet running behind the counter and watching the *sushi* cook make up their orders. Some people prefer to sit at tables and order a made-up selection which is usually cheaper. A good *sushi* bar has the atmosphere of a club, as the regulars behave like members and are well-known to the cooks. Most *sushi* shops have at least three cooks, one of whom will spend most of his time making up the outside orders which are rushed away to neighbouring houses on the back of a bicycle. Saké and beer are the traditional drinks for *sushi*, particularly beer, but today most *sushi* shops are also well stocked with whisky.

Some might ask why *o-sushi* should be included among Japanese crafts. Apart from the skill involved in making *o-sushi*, reflected in the respect with which Japanese treat a good *sushi* cook, the care lavished on the preparation and appearance of all traditional food shows that in Japan craftsmanship is not a limited thing, but can embrace every side of life. To the Japanese, anyone with skill learned by long years of experience and dedication is a craftsman, worthy of respect. Craftsmanship and crafts should be part of everyday life, not limited to special activities or to special occasions. Eastern thought is free of the dualism of the West, and perhaps for this reason the Japanese take a more all-embracing view of life without needing to make endless divisions and distinctions. Craftsmanship should be at the heart of every human occupation for in truth craftsmanship is not what a man does but how he does it. The skilled *sushi* cook is no less a craftsman than the fanmaker since both occupations demand the same human qualities.

96

96 Futaya-san's typical *o-sushi* bar

Making *O-Sushi*

They say it takes five years to make a *sushi*-cook: two years sweeping the floor, and three years learning how to prepare the vinegared rice. This is not as stupid as it sounds for, though without doubt a *sushi*-cook is a kind of craftsman, he is that unusual sort of craftsman who must perform his craft in public and whose performance is in turn an important part of his craft. Hence the importance of the two years sweeping the floor, during which time the young boy-apprentice, for this is a wholly male profession, carefully observes his masters, not only in their handling of rice and raw fish, but in their general style and their close relationship to the customer.

The craft does involve a number of manual skills and dexterities. The making and handling of the special rice is tricky, knives must be kept razor-sharp and each type of fish and other materials must be cut elegantly in the correct way. The handling of the thin sheets of seaweed and the making of

97 The raw fish is sliced

97

'rolls' of different forms also needs skill and experience, not least when all these precarious operations must be done at speed while at the same time carrying on a lively conversation with the customers seated at the bar.

The basic form of *o-sushi* is the slice of raw fish pressed to an elongated ball of sticky rice. Raw tuna, squid, sea bass, bream, abalone, each must be sliced in its correct way, a touch of *wasabi* smeared along the slice, and the fish pressed to exactly the right amount of vinegared and slightly sweetened rice. Handling the sticky rice is easier if one's hands are kept wet with vinegar and water. The finger of *o-sushi* must be firm enough to hold together during the journey from the counter to the saucer of soy sauce to the customer's mouth.

The other main variety of *o-sushi* is *nori maki*, where the *sushi*-rice and other ingredients are rolled in sheets of seaweed in different forms. Extremely popular is the thin kind, often made with tuna, cucumber or conger eel. They are rolled with a small flexible mat made of strips of bamboo closely strung together. The sheet of seaweed is first laid on this and a layer of rice spread over the seaweed, leaving the far edge uncovered. The ingredients, in narrow strips, are placed across the rice and the whole rolled in the mat until the forward edge of the seaweed adheres to the completed roll which is then sliced in knuckle-sized lengths with a wet knife.

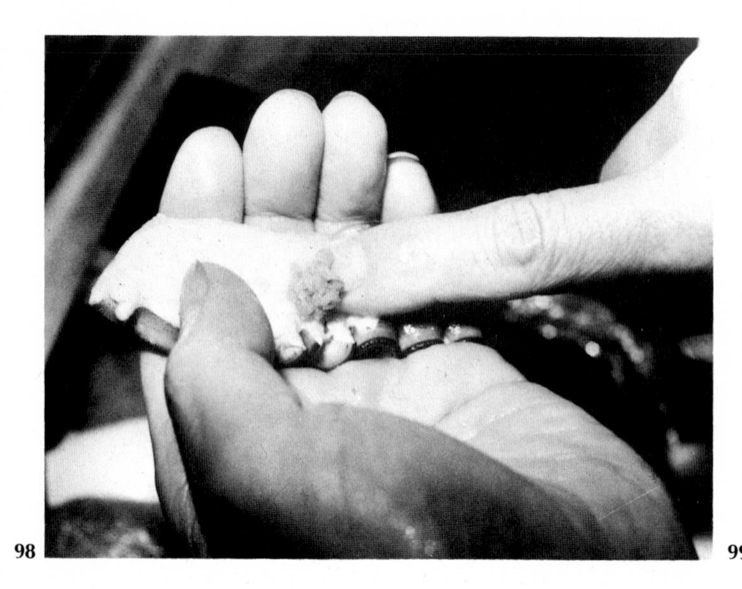

98

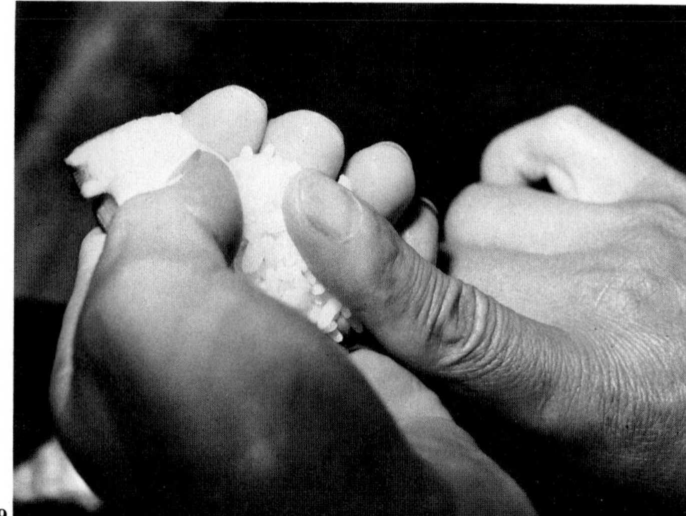

99

98 The fish is smeared with *wasabi*

99 The rice ball is pressed to the fish

100 Finished pieces of finger-*sushi*

100

101 The fish and rice laid out on the seaweed ready for rolling *nori maki*

Practical Note

Probably of all the crafts described in this book, the making of *o-sushi* is the easiest and by no means the least rewarding. Ignore the mystique that surrounds *o-sushi* and try your hand. The ingredients are now all easily available, every kind of fish (totally boned) and many vegetables are suitable and all you really need is practice. Your first finger-*sushi* will probably be rather clumsy and only experiment will show you how you like your rice, but improvement is encouragingly rapid. Most important, keep your hands dampened with vinegared water or within seconds you will be rice-to-the-eyebrows. And finally, never, never, accept from anyone the fact that they do not like raw fish until they have tried it. Almost everyone does!

Bibliography

Adachi, B. *The Living Treasures of Japan*
Wildwood House, London 1973

Akioka, Yoshio *Japanese Knives*. Form and Function Series
Kodansha, Tokyo 1979

Austin, R. *Bamboo*
Weatherhill, Tokyo 1972

Condon, C. *Kites, Crackers and Craftsmen*
Shufunotomo, Tokyo 1974

Dunn, Charles J. *Everyday Life in Traditional Japan*
Tuttle, Tokyo 1981

Hughes, Sukey *Washi, The World of Japanese Paper*
Kodansha, Tokyo 1982

Malm, W. P. *Japanese Music and Musical Instruments*
Tuttle, Tokyo 1973

Massy, Patricia *Sketches of Japanese Crafts*
The Japan Times, Tokyo 1980

Miller, Roy A. *Japan's Modern Myth*
Weatherhill, Tokyo 1982

Munsterberg, H. *Mingei, Folk Arts of Old Japan*
Asia Society, New York 1965

The Folk Arts of Japan
Tuttle, Tokyo 1972

Muraoka, K. *Folk Arts and Crafts of Japan*
Weatherhill/Heibonsha, Tokyo 1973

Nakano, Eisha *Japanese Stencil Dyeing*
Weatherhill, Tokyo 1982

Neptune, John K. *Shakuhachi*
John Neptune, Kyoto 1978

Newman, A. R. *Japanese Art, A Collectors' Guide*
G. Bell, London 1964

Okada, Y. *Japanese Handicrafts*
Japan Travel Bureau, Tokyo 1956

Omae, K. *The Book of Sushi*
Kodansha, Tokyo 1981

Papinot, E. *Historical and Geographical Dictionary of Japan*
Tuttle, Tokyo 1972